A CALL TO STAND APART

A CALL TO STAND APART

Challenging Young Adults to Make an Eternal Difference

Selections From the Writings of
ELLEN G. WHITE

A PARAPHRASE

This book was
Edited by Jeannette R. Johnson
Copyedited by James Cavil
Cover designed by Trent Truman
Interior designed by Tina Ivany
Electronic makeup by Shirely M. Bolivar
Typeset: Bembo 12.6/13.5

PRINTED IN U.S.A.
06 05 04 03 02 5 4 3 2 1

R&H Cataloging Service
White, Ellen Gould Harmon, 1827-1915.
A call to stand apart.

1. Christian life. 2. Religious life. I. Title.
248.4

ISBN 0-8280-1695-X

Contents

Introduction

A Call to Stand Apart is a first. It is the first Ellen White book prepared by the White Estate especially for twenty-first-century young adults. It also is the first book in which a variety of inspired counsels have been drawn together from various previously published Ellen White sources and the language adapted to reach contemporary youth.

A Call to Stand Apart makes available from selected Ellen White writings the core ideas that deal with important issues faced by youth and young adults today. To help communicate successfully with the potentially large audience of youthful readers, sentences and paragraphs have been condensed and language has been modernized. But every effort has been made to be faithful to the content, ideas, and principles set forth by Ellen White. In no case has the thought in the original been changed.

The 17 chapters of the book have been chosen to address issues faced by contemporary young adults in a twenty-first-century context. Each chapter is prefaced by the testimony of a young adult who has found in Ellen White's books the inspiration that he or she would like to have others share.

We believe that the principles penned more than 100 years ago under divine inspiration are more relevant than ever. It is our hope that thousands of readers will find *A Call to Stand Apart* so compelling, interesting, and inspiring that they will go on to explore the deep spiritual riches found in Ellen White's standard writings. May each reader "catch the vision."

—The Trustees of the
Ellen G. White Publications

JUST JESUS AND YOU

CHAPTER 1

BEGINNINGS

A YOUNG ADULT'S ENCOUNTER WITH ELLEN WHITE . . . ON SALVATION

Ellen White makes the topics of salvation and the love of Christ, who died for me, both simple and personal. When I open The Desire of Ages, *He's right there. He's so real, so able to save.*

When I read what Ellen White says about the topic of salvation, it's like no other author. What she writes has to do with me personally. It's my life she's talking about—my feelings and experiences. I recognize them. This is a salvation of experience, one I can touch, because it's about Jesus. I know she knew Jesus personally. Whatever any other writer knew, it doesn't compare with this.

Other writers may have something important to say, they may try to share the right ideas, but in the pages of The Desire of Ages *Ellen White is trying to share salvation through Jesus. And the best thing is she makes me want it! I want it with all my heart.*

In her writings she talks about salvation in the real world—my world. It's not about only ideas. It's not a beehive of rhetoric. The intellectual part has its place, but when I get up in the morning to face my day spiritually, what I want needs to be clear, vivid, and personal. I find that in her writings. My strength to save myself is like "ropes of sand," as she puts it. I know she's right because I've felt those ropes crumble in my hands. What she describes I can touch, for it's a theology of flesh and blood. It's about Jesus! Ellen

White paints a picture of a Christ as someone who is real, who is able to save me from myself.

Most of all, I know she has written because she wanted me to be saved and not because she wanted me to believe her ideas. And I do want to be saved, with all my heart. I want to know Christ and the power of His resurrection and the fellowship of sharing in His sufferings, becoming like Him in His death, and so, somehow, to attain to the resurrection from the dead.

—Laura, age 24

A Young Adult's Encounter With Ellen White . . . on Salvation

"Christ, the heavenly merchantman seeking goodly pearls, saw in lost humanity the pearl of price. In men and women, defiled and ruined by sin, He saw the possibilities of redemption."[1]

As a child I always fancied pearls. I loved their gentle curves and soft off-white luster.

I thought they were prettier than any diamond or ruby could ever be. So it didn't surprise me that Ellen White compared our beloved Savior to my favorite jewel. What I didn't expect was that she wrote that Christ saw in lost humanity "the pearl of price." How could He find something so beautiful in me? But when I read her eloquent illustrations further I understood what, for me, is the true essence of salvation. Christ doesn't seek me because I am lost. He doesn't long to save me because He feels obliged to. He gives me salvation because He loves me.

Mrs. White thoughtfully wrote of Christ, our heavenly merchantman. Reading what she writes makes me rejoice daily for humanity because He finds the precious pearls He is seeking in our old, marred earth—because He sees the pearl in me.

—Jennifer, age 22

BEGINNINGS

Now the birth of Jesus the Messiah took place in this way. When his mother Mary had been engaged to Joseph, but before they lived together, she was found to be with child from the Holy Spirit. Her husband Joseph, being a righteous man and unwilling to expose her to public disgrace, planned to dismiss her quietly. But just when he had resolved to do this, an angel of the Lord appeared to him in a dream and said, "Joseph, son of David, do not be afraid to take Mary as your wife, for the child conceived in her is from the Holy Spirit. She will bear a son, and you are to name him Jesus, for he will save his people from their sins."

All this took place to fulfill what had been spoken by the Lord through the prophet: "Look, the virgin shall conceive and bear a son, and they shall name him Emmanuel," which means, "God is with us." When Joseph awoke from sleep, he did as the angel of the Lord commanded him; he took her as his wife, but had no marital relations with her until she had borne a son; and he named him Jesus (Matthew 1:18-25).

In that region there were shepherds living in the fields, keeping watch over their flock by night. Then an angel of the Lord stood before them, and the glory of the Lord shone around them, and they were terrified. But the angel said to them, "Do not be afraid; for see—I am bringing you good news of great joy for all the people: to you is born this day in the city of David a Savior, who is the Messiah, the Lord. This will be a sign for you: you will find a child wrapped in bands of cloth and lying in a manger." And suddenly there was with the angel a multitude of the heavenly host, praising God and saying, "Glory to God in the highest heaven, and on earth peace among those whom he favors!"

When the angels had left them and gone into heaven, the shepherds said to one another, "Let us go now to Bethlehem and see this thing that has taken place, which the Lord has made known to us." So they went with haste and found Mary and Joseph, and the child lying in the manger. When they saw this, they made known what had been told them about this child: and all who heard it were amazed at what the shepherds told them. But Mary treasured all these words and pondered them in her heart. The shepherds returned, glorifying and praising God for all they had heard and seen, as it had been told them (Luke 2:8-20).

The promise that Jesus would come as our Savior had been made in the Garden of Eden. When Adam and Eve first heard it, they expected a quick fulfillment. So when they held their firstborn son in their arms, they both hoped he would be the Redeemer. But that was not to be. Thousands of years later, as God's appointed time came, Jesus left heaven to be born in Bethlehem.[2]

In becoming human, Jesus demonstrated ultimate humility. On earth His physical surroundings were primitive. He hid His glory from those who saw Him and shunned all outward display. The angels marveled at such a plan of redemption and watched to see how the people of God would receive His Son.[3]

The Roman decree to register everyone in the vast empire extended to the humble people living in the hills of Galilee. Angels watched over Joseph and Mary as they journeyed from their home in Nazareth south to Bethlehem. When the two arrived in Bethlehem, weary and homeless, they walked the length of the main street, from the gate of the city to the eastern end of the town, seeking a place to spend the night. But there was no room for them anywhere! Finally, in a crude animal shelter, they found a place to lie down, and Mary gave birth to her son, the Redeemer of the world.[4]

Above the hills of Bethlehem an immense throng of angels had gathered for this moment, and at His birth they began to sing this great news to the world. Unfortunately, the religious leadership in Israel, ignoring their destiny, did not share in the celebration.[5]

In the same fields where David once cared for his father's flocks, shepherds guarded their sheep through the night. They had been talking of the promised Savior and praying for His coming. Then suddenly an angel said to them, "Do not be afraid. I bring you good news of great joy that will be for all the people. Today in the town of David a Savior has been born to you; he is Christ the Lord" (Luke 2:10, 11, NIV). The whole area was lighted up with the brightness of the angels.[6]

When the angels disappeared, the light faded away, and darkness returned to the hills around Bethlehem. But the brightest picture ever seen by human eyes remained in the memory of the shepherds. When they regained their composure, they said, " 'Let's go to Bethlehem and see this thing that has happened, which the Lord has told us about.' So they hurried off and found Mary and Joseph, and the baby, who was lying in the manger" (Luke 2:15, 16, NIV).[7]

Heaven and earth are no wider apart today than when shepherds heard the angels' song. And each of us now, as the shepherds then, is the object of God's most intense love and interest.[8]

The story of Bethlehem is a fantastic theme. We should marvel that Jesus exchanged the throne of heaven and the worship of angels for a manger bed and the company of sheep and goats. Yet this was only the beginning of the evidence of His great love. It would have been the ultimate humiliation for Jesus to take Adam's nature, even when he stood in his innocence in Eden. But Jesus accepted humanity when the race had been weakened by millennia of sin. Like every other human baby, He accepted the results of the laws of heredity so He would be able to share and understand our disappointments and temptations, and to give us the example of what it means to live a perfect life.[9]

CHAPTER 2

Jesus as a Child and Young Adult

The child grew and became strong, filled with wisdom; and the favor of God was upon him. Now every year his parents went to Jerusalem for the festival of the Passover. And when he was twelve years old, they went up as usual for the festival. When the festival was ended and they started to return, the boy Jesus stayed behind in Jerusalem, but his parents did not know it. Assuming that he was in the group of travelers, they went a day's journey. Then they started to look for him among their relatives and friends. When they did not find him, they returned to Jerusalem to search for him. After three days they found him in the temple, sitting among the teachers, listening to them and asking them questions. And all who heard him were amazed at his understanding and his answers. When his parents saw him they were astonished; and his mother said to him, "Child, why have you treated us like this? Look, your father and I have been searching for you in great anxiety." He said to them, "Why were you searching for me? Did you not know that I must be in my Father's house?" But they did not understand what he said to them. Then he went down with them and came to Nazareth, and was obedient to them. His mother treasured all these things in her heart. And Jesus increased in wisdom and in years, and in divine and human favor (Luke 2:40-52).

From their earliest years, Jewish children were surrounded by rabbis and their rigid rules for everything down to the smallest detail. But Jesus didn't show any interest in those ways. From childhood He acted independently from such restrictions. He constantly studied the Old Testament and gradually became aware of the spiritual condition of the people in His village. He observed that the standards of society and the standards of God were in constant conflict. People would forget God's words and observe their own traditions that had no value.[10]

In His gentle way Jesus tried to please those around Him. The scribes misunderstood this gentleness and assumed He would be easily influenced by their teachings. But when they questioned Him, He asked for their authority from the Bible. He seemed to know the Scriptures from beginning to end. The rabbis were ashamed of being instructed by a child and indignant at His opposition. They soon realized that Jesus' spiritual understanding was far beyond theirs.[11]

At a very early age Jesus began to act for Himself in the formation of character, and not even respect and love for His parents could turn Him from obedience to God. The words of Scripture became the reason for everything He did that was different from the family's customs. His brothers, Joseph's sons, sided with the rabbis, insisting that traditions had to be followed the same as the laws of God. They called Jesus' strict obedience to the laws of God "stubbornness." They were astounded at His knowledge and wisdom when answering the rabbis and recognized that His education had to come from a higher source than theirs.[12]

There were some who wanted to be friends with Jesus because they felt at peace with Him; but more of His peers avoided Him because they felt condemned by such a pure life. He was bright and cheerful; His friends enjoyed His company and welcomed His suggestions. But they were impatient with His scruples and called Him narrow and straitlaced.[13]

Jesus' choices were a continuous mystery to His parents

from the time they found Him in the temple at age 12. For example, His happiest hours were spent alone with nature and with God. Early in the morning He would go to a quiet place to meditate, read the Bible, and pray. Then He would return home to do the family chores. He loved to help suffering persons, and even suffering animals.[14]

Jesus found value in every person. He went out of His way to speak kind words of encouragement to sick, oppressed, and discouraged persons. Sometimes He even gave hungry people His own lunch. He tried to bring the hope of spiritual victory and the assurance of being part of God's family to everyone, including the rough and unpromising. Jesus never contended for His own rights, even though He was harassed and was often treated unfairly.[15]

At times His mother Mary wavered between Jesus and His brothers, who didn't believe Jesus had been sent from God. But they could hardly deny His divine character or the fact that His presence brought a pure atmosphere into their home.[16]

CHAPTER 3

JESUS' MINISTRY BEGINS WITH A PARTY

On the third day there was a marriage in Cana in Galilee, and the mother of Jesus was there; Jesus also was invited to the marriage, with his disciples. When the wine failed, the mother of Jesus said to him, "They have no wine." And Jesus said to her, "O woman, what have you to do with me? My hour has not yet come." His mother said to the servants, "Do whatever he tells you." Now six stone jars were standing there, for the Jewish rites of purification, each holding twenty or thirty gallons. Jesus said to them, "Fill the jars with water." And they filled them up to the brim. He said to them, "Now draw some out, and take it to the steward of the feast." So they took it. When the steward of the feast tasted the water now become wine, and did not know where it came from (though the servants who had drawn the water knew), the steward of the feast called the bridegroom and said to him, "Every man serves the good wine first; and when men have drunk freely, then the poor wine; but you have kept the good wine until now." This, the first of his signs, Jesus did at Cana in Galilee, and manifested his glory; and his disciples believed in him (John 2:1-11, RSV).

About age 30 Jesus began His public ministry, but not at the religious headquarters in Jerusalem. He started at a wedding reception in a small village in Galilee. Jesus showed from the start that He wanted people to be happy. In Cana, a village close to Nazareth, some relatives of Joseph and

Mary invited them to the party. Jesus, who had been away from home for some weeks, joined them and brought His recently called disciples with Him.[17]

A quiet anticipation and excitement filled the air as small groups of guests discussed Jesus. Mary was proud of her Son. While they had been separated, she had heard reports of His baptism in the Jordan River by John the Baptist, and it brought back to her mind many memories. From the day she heard the angel's announcement of Jesus' birth in her home at Nazareth, she had treasured each evidence that Jesus was the Messiah. His continuously unselfish life convinced her that He could be no one else. Yet she also experienced doubts and disappointments and longed for the time when He would finally show His divinity. By now, death had separated Mary from Joseph, who had shared her knowledge of the mystery of the birth of Jesus. So she had no one in whom to confide. The past weeks had been especially difficult.[18]

At the marriage feast she saw the same tender Son she had raised. Yet she could tell He had changed. She saw the evidences of the cruel temptations in the wilderness and a new sense of dignity and power as He walked and talked. A group of men accompanied Him. Their eyes followed Him constantly, reverently, and they called Him "Master." These men told Mary what they had seen and heard at His baptism and elsewhere. They concluded with what Philip told Nathanial: "We have found the one Moses wrote about in the Law, and about whom the prophets also wrote—Jesus of Nazareth, the son of Joseph" (John 1:45, NIV).[19]

As Mary saw the many glances of the guests in Jesus' direction, she longed to have Him prove His Messiahship. She hoped and prayed He might perform a miracle. At that time marriage festivities continued for several days, and at this wedding the wine ran out before the party ended. As a relative of the bride and groom, Mary was among the caterers, so she commented pointedly to Jesus, "They have no wine." It was an undisguised suggestion for Him to do something dramatic.[20]

Jesus' answer, "My hour is not yet come," indicated that no earthly ties would dictate His conduct. Though Mary did not fully understand her Son's mission, she trusted Him implicitly. And Jesus responded to that faith. He also acted to strengthen the faith of His disciples by performing His first miracle.[21]

Beside the doorway stood six large stone water jars. Jesus directed the servants to fill them with water. And because the guests needed to be served immediately, He told them to take some of the contents to the person in charge of the gathering. When they did, instead of the water with which they had filled the jars, they poured wine! Hardly anyone knew the original wine supply had run out, but when the wedding coordinator tasted what his servants brought, he knew it to be far superior to any he had drunk thus far at the wedding. Turning to the bridegroom, he said, "Everyone man serves the good wine first; and when men have drunk freely, then the poor wine; but you have kept the good wine until now" (John 2:10).[22]

The "wine" of the partying that you and I do ultimately turns sour. But the gifts of Jesus are always fresh. What He provides for us always satisfies and brings us happiness. Each new gift we receive increases our capacity to receive more and enjoy more from Him. He gives grace and still more grace and, unlike the wine at Cana, His supply of blessings never runs short and is never exhausted. Actually, the gift of Jesus to the marriage party is a wonderful symbol. The water in the jars represents His "baptism into death," and the wine represents His blood spilled for us to cleanse us from sin. At this first feast with His disciples, Jesus gave them a cup of wine to symbolize His work for their salvation. And at the Last Supper He gave it to them again and invited them to drink it in this symbolic way until He returns.[23]

CHAPTER 4

YOU CAN COME HOME ANY TIME

Then Jesus said, "There was a man who had two sons. The younger of them said to his father, 'Father, give me the share of the property that will belong to me.' So he divided his property between them. A few days later the younger son gathered all he had and traveled to a distant country, and there he squandered his property in dissolute living. When he had spent everything, a severe famine took place throughout that country, and he began to be in need. So he went and hired himself out to one of the citizens of that country, who sent him to his fields to feed the pigs. He would gladly have filled himself with the pods that the pigs were eating; and no one gave him anything. But when he came to himself he said, 'How many of my father's hired hands have bread enough and to spare, but here I am dying of hunger! I will get up and go to my father, and I will say to him, "Father, I have sinned against heaven and before you; I am no longer worthy to be called your son; treat me like one of your hired hands."' So he set off and went to his father. But while he was still far off, his father saw him and was filled with compassion; he ran and put his arms around him and kissed him. Then the son said to him, 'Father, I have sinned against heaven and before you; I am no longer worthy to be called your son.' But the father said to his slaves, 'Quickly, bring out a robe—the best one—and put it on him; put a ring on his finger and sandals on his feet. And get the fatted calf and kill it, and let us eat and celebrate; for this son of mine was dead and is alive again; he was lost and is found!' And they began to celebrate.

Now his elder son was in the field; and when he came and approached the house, he heard music and dancing. He called one of the slaves and asked what was going on. He replied, 'Your brother has come, and your father has killed the fatted calf, because he has got him back safe and sound.' Then he became angry and refused to go in. His father came out and began to plead with him. But he answered his father, 'Listen! For all these years I have been working like a slave for you, and I have never disobeyed your command; yet you have never given me even a young goat so that I might celebrate with my friends. But when this son of yours came back, who has devoured your property with prostitutes, you killed the fatted calf for him!' Then the father said to him, 'Son, you are always with me, and all that is mine is yours. But we had to celebrate and rejoice, because this brother of yours was dead and has come to life; he was lost and has been found'" (Luke 15:11-32).

This is the story of a young man weary of the restraints of living at home.[24]

Things came to the point that he decided he had to get away. His wealthy loving father gave the lad his inheritance, and he left for a place he thought he would have freedom to do whatever he pleased. He had the money to satisfy every desire. Because money attracts company, he soon had a group of friends to help him spend his wealth in high living.

But the hopes and dreams he had nurtured while a boy at home soon sank into oblivion, along with the stability and security of his spiritual upbringing. His inheritance squandered, he applied for a job and was assigned to look after hogs. For a Jew, nothing could have been worse. Jesus' Jewish audience understood the pits of degradation and humiliation He was describing. The young man, determined to find liberty, instead found himself a virtual slave. Friendless, starving, and sick at heart, he forced himself to eat hogs' food to survive.[25]

In this narrative we see an amazing picture of the hopelessness of a life divorced from God. It may take time for us to realize how poverty-stricken we are when we separate ourselves from the love of the heavenly Father, but that day will come. All the while, God is desperately seeking to find ways to influence us to return home.

The young man ultimately came to his senses, realizing that the servants in his father's house were better off than he was. In his misery, the boy remembered his father's love. And the memories of that love began to beckon him home.

Finally, he made the decision to head back and to confess his waywardness. He decides he will tell his father, "I've sinned against heaven and you; I'm not worthy to be called your son, but let me be like one of your employees." Weak from hunger in a land of famine, with only rags left for clothes, he finally left the pigpens and set out for the place he grew up as a child.[26]

The runaway had no conception of the sadness that had overwhelmed his father when he left. He never dreamed of the shadow that came over the whole house when reports filtered back of his wild partying. And no one could have convinced him that every day his father sat, watching, waiting, for his son's return. Yet now, with weary and painful steps, he turned eagerly toward home to beg for a servant's position.

While still a considerable distance from the house, the father recognized his son and ran to meet him, hugging him in a long, clinging, emotional embrace. To protect his son from being observed in such a destitute condition, the father took off his own beautiful coat and placed it around the boy's shoulders.[27]

Overcome by such a loving reception, the young man began to sob his repentance speech. But the father would hear none of it. He had no place in his household for a servant-son; his lad must have the very best the house could provide. The father told his servants to bring the finest clothes and a ring for his hand, to find fine shoes for his feet and to prepare a feast so everyone could celebrate. And there would be a theme at this celebration: "The dead son is alive; the lost son has been found."

What a vastly different perception this boy now had of his father! He had always thought of him as rather stern and severe. But no longer. In his great need he saw the true character of his father. Which is what this story is all about. In our rebellion, we often think of God as severe and stern, demanding in His requirements. But when you have been away a long time and are spiritually hungry, dressed in the rags of sin and guilt, then you'll see how fully loving and accepting the heavenly Father really is. When you take even one step toward your Father in repentance, He will run to wrap you in His arms of love. He will forgive your sins and never remember them again (Jeremiah 31:34).[28]

Don't wait or try to clean yourself up so you can be good enough to come to Jesus. If we waited to be good enough, we would never come. Jesus is waiting for you, calling you, yearning for you. All heaven will celebrate when you come home.[29]

CHAPTER 5

WHEN DOING EVERYTHING RIGHT ISN'T ENOUGH

Then someone came to him and said, "Teacher, what good deed must I do to have eternal life?" And he said to him, "Why do you ask me about what is good? There is only one who is good. If you wish to enter into life, keep the commandments." He said to him, "Which ones?" And Jesus said, "You shall not murder; You shall not commit adultery; You shall not steal; You shall not bear false witness; Honor your father and mother; also, You shall love your neighbor as yourself." The young man said to him, "I have kept all these; what do I still lack?" Jesus said to him, "If you wish to be perfect, go, sell your possessions, and give the money to the poor, and you will have treasure in heaven; then come, follow me" (Matthew 19:16-22).

This young man had what many people of his age seem to want—position and wealth. One day, watching Jesus' tender and affectionate interaction with children, he found growing in his heart the desire to be the Lord's disciple. The idea became so urgent that he ran after Jesus, knelt down, and earnestly asked the most important question in life: "Good Master, what can I do to have eternal life?"

Jesus responded with a challenge that probed the youth's thoughts. He replied, "Only God is good, so why do you call Me good?

This young executive obviously lived "the good life."

He'd convinced himself that he had "made it" in both the workplace and in his spiritual life. Yet, for all that, he sensed something was missing. He had seen the way Jesus blessed children and wanted Jesus to bless him, too.

In reply to his question, Jesus told him to keep the commandments and quoted a few of them that deal with our interpersonal relationships. The young ruler replied with certainty that he'd done it all since his youth. Then he added the poignant question "What is missing?" As Jesus looked in the young man's face, He searched his life and character. He loved the youth kneeling at His feet and wanted to give him the peace he desired. So He replied, "One thing is missing. Sell all your possessions and give the proceeds to the poor. That will give you a bank account in heaven. Then pick up the cross and follow Me."[30]

Jesus sincerely wanted this young man as one of His disciples. He knew the youth could be a tremendous influence for good. He had many fine qualifications and talents. Jesus wanted to give him the opportunity to develop a character that would reflect the likeness of God.

If the ruler had joined Jesus, he would have been a great power for good. If he'd made the choice to be a disciple, how different his life would have been.[31]

His life could have become all he wanted it to be. But one thing was missing, just one! To sell and distribute his great wealth and join Jesus would have corrected that one weakness. That action would have emptied self-interest from his life and filled it instead with the love of God. Jesus asked him to make a choice between worldly wealth and heavenly worth.

To join Jesus meant that this young man had to accept a life of self-denial. With deep interest Jesus watched him weigh the question. With keen insight the ruler understood what he'd been told, but it made him depressed. If he had sensed what he would gain in the gift Jesus offered, he would have become a disciple. Instead, he reflected on what he would lose.[32]

The man kneeling before Jesus served as an honored member of a council of the Jews, and Satan tempted him to think of the flattering prospects that position held. Yes, to be sure, this young adult did want the spiritual treasure Jesus offered. But he also wanted the advantages of his wealth. Yes, he desired eternal life. But he didn't want all that sacrifice. Finally, having thought it through, he walked away in great sadness. The cost of eternal life seemed too high.

The rich young ruler became a victim of self-deception. Even though he said otherwise, he hadn't been keeping all the commandments. He had an idol that he worshiped—his wealth. He loved his possessions more than God, the gifts more than the Giver.

Many today face the same choice. They weigh the competing claims of the spiritual world and the material world. And like the young ruler, they turn away from Jesus and say, "I can't serve this Man."[33]

If only he'd been able to see beyond a life of lawkeeping to the life of true loving that Jesus offered, how different his life might have been.

The ruler had been given much so he could demonstrate generosity. It's the same today. God gives us talents and opportunities to work with Him in helping the poor and suffering. Whenever we use our gifts this way, we partner with God to win others for Christ. Those who enjoy positions of great influence and financial security may think the cost to follow Jesus is too great. But self-surrender is at the very heart of what it means to be His follower. Often this reality is expressed in language that sounds demanding, but God has no other way to save us except to separate us from whatever will ultimately destroy us.[34]

Jesus called another wealthy man to His service who

did leave all, exchanging his lucrative business for poverty and hardship.[35]

No one likes the "tax man." Not today, and not in the times of Christ in Palestine. Those officials were the most reviled of all. Not only because they collected taxes (a painful reminder to the Jews of their Roman conquerors), but also because these men were dishonest. Through extortion they made themselves wealthy. And when a Jew worked for the Romans collecting taxes, he was viewed as part of the vilest segment of their society.[36]

Matthew was one of the hated extortionists. But one day that all changed. After calling two sets of brothers by the Sea of Galilee, Peter and Andrew, then James and John, Jesus called Matthew to be His disciple. While others judged Matthew by his vocation, Jesus read his heart and recognized that it was open. Matthew had heard Jesus speak and wanted to ask for help but had convinced himself that the Great Teacher would never notice him.[37]

Sitting at his tax desk one day, Matthew saw Jesus approaching. Moments later he was astonished to hear Jesus say, "Follow Me." Matthew stood up from his desk, left everything as it was, turned away, and followed Jesus. He didn't hesitate, didn't question, didn't give a moment's thought to his lucrative business or the poverty he was about to receive in exchange. For Matthew, it was enough to be with Jesus, to listen to His words, and to work with Him.

It happened the same way with the brothers Jesus had just called. Peter and Andrew heard the call, dropped their nets on the beach, left their fishing boat, and walked away with Jesus. They didn't ask how they would make a living or support their families. The call to be His disciple they found too compelling to rationalize or postpone. They simply obeyed the call and joined Jesus.

Reports of Matthew's action created citywide interest.

And in the exuberance of his new discipleship, Matthew desperately sought to influence his former associates. So he organized a party at his house and invited relatives and friends. Those friends included not only tax collectors but also many other people of "doubtful reputation," people strictly avoided by their more scrupulous neighbors.

But Jesus didn't hesitate to accept the invitation, even though He knew it would offend the Jewish leaders and place Him in a dubious position in the eyes of others. With pleasure Jesus attended the dinner party, where Matthew seated Him at the head table surrounded by dishonest tax collectors.[38]

During the party some rabbis tried to turn the new disciples against their new Master by asking, "Why does your Master eat with tax men and sinners?" Jesus overheard the question, and before His disciples could answer He challenged the rabbis with the words: "Healthy people don't go to the doctor, only the sick. Why don't you go and try to work out the meaning of these words, 'I would have mercy, not sacrifice.' I haven't come to call the self-righteous. I have come to call sinners to repent."

The Pharisees claimed to be spiritually complete, with no need of a spiritual physician. They considered tax collectors and Gentiles as dying from their soul diseases. So Jesus confronted these religious leaders with an obvious truth: Why would He not associate with the very people that needed His help?[39]

A legal religion can never attract anyone to Jesus. It's so devoid of love! Fasting and prayer motivated by a self-justifying spirit are abominable. Even solemn religious services, religious ceremonies, the public "humiliation" of self, and impressive sacrifices intended to show that a person is "entitled" to heaven are a complete deception. Nothing we can do can ever purchase salvation.[40]

In the final analysis, it is only when we renounce our

self-interest that we can become a believer, a follower, a disciple of Jesus. The rich young ruler couldn't bring himself to do it. Matthew did. One made the right choice; the other didn't. Matthew was converted and entered a life of joy-filled service. The other continued a life of human prestige, wealth—and emptiness. One found eternal life; the other missed it. When we renounce self-interest, the Lord animates us with new life. Only "new bottles" can contain the "new wine" of a life renewed in Christ.[41]

CHAPTER 6

THE ANSWER LIES IN THE SOIL

That same day Jesus went out of the house and sat beside the lake. Such great crowds gathered around him that he got into a boat and sat there, while the whole crowd stood on the beach. And he told them many things in parables, saying: "Listen! A sower went out to sow. And as he sowed, some seeds fell on the path, and the birds came and ate them up. Other seeds fell on rocky ground, where they did not have much soil, and they sprang up quickly, since they had no depth of soil. But when the sun rose, they were scorched; and since they had no root, they withered away. Other seeds fell among thorns, and the thorns grew up and choked them. Other seeds fell on good soil and brought forth grain, some a hundredfold, some sixty, some thirty. Let anyone with ears listen!"

"Hear then the parable of the sower. When anyone hears the word of the kingdom and does not understand it, the evil one comes and snatches away what is sown in the heart; this is what was sown on the path. As for what was sown on rocky ground, this is the one who hears the word and immediately receives it with joy; yet such a person has no root, but endures only for a while, and when trouble or persecution arises on account of the word, that person immediately falls away. As for what was sown among thorns, this is the one who hears the word, but the cares of the world and the lure of wealth choke the word, and it yields nothing. But as for what was sown on good soil, this is the one who hears the word and understands it, who indeed bears fruit and

yields, in one case a hundredfold, in another sixty, and in another thirty" (Matthew 13:1-9, 18-23).

A crowd had gathered by the Sea of Galilee, eager to see and hear Jesus. Among them were many sick hoping to be healed. It was a joy for Jesus to exercise His right to restore them to vibrant health.[42]

As the crowd grew larger and pressed closer, Jesus finally had no room on the beach. So He stepped into a fishing boat and asked the disciples to push out a little into the water. Unhindered, He then spoke to the crowd listening on the shore.

The plain of Gennesaret stretched out beside the lakeshore, and beyond it rose the hills. That day, on both the plain and the hillsides, workers were busy. Some were planting grain; others were reaping a harvest from an early crop. Jesus, seeing these activities, told the farmer/seed parable.

The Jews of that day were fixated on a Messiah who would reestablish their earthly kingdom. But Jesus explained that the kingdom would not be established by force, violence, or weapons of war. It would come only when a startling new principle found fertile soil in human minds.[43]

To set the stage for understanding this truth, Jesus presented Himself in the story, not as a powerful king but as a humble farmer planting seeds. In this way He taught them that the same laws that control planting, growth, and harvesting on a farm also apply to the development of our spiritual lives.[44]

The story left the crowd mystified. It awakened their interest, but it also dashed their dreams. Even the disciples failed to get the point of the parable. They privately came to Jesus later and asked for an explanation.[45]

In the words of the promise made to Adam and Eve in Eden, Jesus planted the seed of the gospel. And in the words of this parable Jesus again planted the seed of the gospel. In the story, the seed represents the word of God. Every seed contains life. And every word from God contains life. Jesus said, "Anyone who hears my word and believes him who sent me has eternal life, and does not come under judgment, but has passed from death to life" (John 5:24). The life of God is in every requirement and promise of the Word of God. Through Him every requirement is accomplished and every promise becomes reality. So to receive God's Word is to receive the life and character of God.

All seeds reproduce themselves—and only themselves. If you plant seeds under receptive conditions, then the specific life in that seed will grow. In the same way, if you plant the words of God in your life under receptive conditions, they will grow a life and character like the life and character of God.[46] Philosophy and secular literature, no matter how brilliant, can't do this. But when God's words are planted in your soul, they spring to life, everlasting life.[47]

Note that in the story the farmer sowed his seed. Jesus taught truth because He is the truth. His own thoughts, character, and life-experience permeated His teaching. And the same principle applies whenever we share God's Word with others. We can teach effectively only what we have experienced. So before we share the good news, we must make it our own by personal experience.

The story of the farmer describes four contrasting situations, four kinds of places on which the seed fell. When the farmer scattered the seed by hand, the breeze could take it in any direction, some intended and some not. Jesus told the story so His hearers would understand that the results are determined exclusively by the conditions into which the seed falls.

Some seed fell on packed pathways. Jesus explained it this way: "Some [seeds] fell along the path, and the birds came and ate it up" (Matthew 13:4, NIV). The seed that falls on the beaten path is a symbol of God's Word that comes to an unresponsive heart. There is much traffic on this path—sinful types of pleasure, selfish career goals, worldly indulgences. Time and attention are completely absorbed, and no attention is given to the words that bring life.

And just as birds are quick to see and feed on scattered seed, so temptation comes to divert our attention and make us indifferent. And if this reaction continues, soon our heart becomes like that hard path where the seeds of the gospel were scattered. It is unreceptive and calloused."

Jesus continued: "Other seeds fell on rocky ground, where they did not have much soil, and they sprang up quickly, since they had no depth of soil. But when the sun rose they were scorched; and since they had no root, they withered away" (Matthew 13:5, 6).[48]

If you plant some seeds in your window box or a stone pot filled with a little soil and mostly stones, you'll see them sprout. But in the heat of the day, if plants have no root system and can't access the nutrients and moisture of the soil, they quickly wither. This is a symbol of the reaction of some to receiving God's Word. There is a profession of interest, an external reaching out to God but, like the rich young ruler, they trust in their own good works instead of the strength and power of the Lord. Self-interest continues to remain the active principle of life. There can be intellectual conviction, superficiality of action, but no true heart conviction, which means it soon comes to nothing.

Remember Matthew's reaction to hearing the words of Jesus? He considered the invitation, counted the cost, and, without delay, got up, left everything, and followed Him. But the seed that falls in "rocky places" represents those who act rashly. They don't count the cost; they act impulsively. They don't make a full commitment to the Lord Jesus or to living the life He offers. They are content to live with external appearances without making changes in their destructive habit patterns.[49]

And the hot summer sun that strengthens and ripens healthy plants destroys plants that have no root system. Some people accept the gospel as a way out of personal difficulties rather than as a deliverance from sin. They're happy for a time thinking that religion will solve their problems. And as long as life moves along smoothly, they appear to be consistent Christians. But they faint when confronted by the first fiery temptation.[50]

Love is the principle of God's government, and it must be the foundation of a Christian's character. Nothing else can give us the strength to overcome trial and temptation.[51] And that love is revealed in sacrifice. The plan of redemption was born in sacrifice, and God's loving sacrifice is immeasurable. Jesus gave all for us, and those who receive Him will be ready to sacrifice all for Him.

Jesus says, "Other seeds fell among thorns, and the thorns grew up and choked them" (Matthew 13:7). You can't grow a crop of wheat among weeds and thorns. And the seeds of God's love can thrive only when what otherwise "grows naturally" is rooted out, allowing God's grace to be the active principle in your life. As long as the Holy Spirit is allowed to work, our characters will be refined, and we will find the strength to weed out the habits that are in opposition to God's will. Accepting Jesus must be followed by modeling Him. It's a process the Bible calls sanctification. The two must always go together.

Jesus was quite specific in naming the factors that can keep us from growing in Him. One factor He identified as "the cares of the world." This applies to all people, no matter what their social situation. The poor fear they will not be able to obtain their basic necessities. The rich fear they will lose what they have accumulated. The fears of us all about security should lead us to the One who has promised to supply all our needs, for He cares for us. No matter where we work or spend our time, we can become so absorbed in secular pursuits that we squeeze out of our lives those essentials for the growth of the seed of God's Word—time to meditate about God and heaven, time to pray, time to study Scripture, time to seek and serve God. The noise of the world overpowers the voice of the Spirit of God.

Next, Jesus talked about the deceitfulness of wealth. Instead of regarding wealth as a gift to be used for God's glory and for helping others, it can be used as a means of promoting self. In this case, instead of developing the selflessness of God, we develop the selfishness of Satan.[52]

Then Jesus talked about "the pleasures of life." He didn't mean we were not to have a good time. (After all, He began His ministry in Palestine at a wedding celebration and didn't hesitate to attend social gatherings such as Matthew's and Simon's.) Rather, here Jesus discusses the danger of those kinds of amusements that draw our affections away from Him. He's condemning indulgences that diminish our physical strength, dull our minds, and numb our spiritual perceptions—all of which stifle spiritual growth.

The farmer, Jesus continued, does not always meet with disappointment. Sometimes the seed falls into good ground, and he reaps a wonderful harvest. "But as for what was sown on good soil, this is the one who hears the word and understands it" (Matthew 13:23). This doesn't refer to a heart without sin, because the Gospel is to be preached to the lost. Rather, the honest heart refers to one who yields to the conviction of the Holy Spirit, confessing guilt, feeling the need of the mercy and love of God. The person who receives the Scriptures as the voice of God is the true learner. Angels of God come close to those who humbly seek for divine guidance.[53]

If our hearts become the "good ground," we will choose

to fill our minds with great thoughts, pure thoughts. Jesus will live in us, producing the good fruit of obedience and good works. Our troubles and difficulties will help us become more Christ like until we seek eternal life with our whole heart, even at the cost of loss, persecution, or death itself.[54]

Throughout the story of the farmer, Jesus showed that the differing planting results are based on the receptivity of the soil. In each case the farmer is the same, and the seed is the same. So if the Word of God fails to prosper in our lives, the problem lies in ourselves. The results are in our control. It's true that we can't change ourselves; but we do have the power of choice, so we determine what we will become. If your experience has been that of a beaten pathway or stony ground, thorns, and weeds, it doesn't have to continue that way.[55]

God's Spirit is ready to break the old patterns and to give you a new life if you will allow your heart to be "good soil," a hearer and a doer of His Word.

As the seed of His Word grows roots deep into the fertile soil of your heart, it will sprout! By the invisible union of your life with Jesus, through faith your spiritual life can flourish. When Jesus plants the seeds of the good news in the receptive soil of your heart, the harvest is joy—joy for you, joy for all of heaven![56]

CHAPTER 7

How to Pray

"And whenever you pray, do not be like the hypocrites, for they love to stand and pray in the synagogues and at the street corners, so that they may be seen by others. Truly I tell you, they have received their reward. But whenever you pray, go into your room and shut the door and pray to your Father who is in secret; and your Father who sees you in secret will reward you. When you are praying, do not heap up empty phrases as the Gentiles do; for they think that they will be heard because of their many words. Do not be like them, for your Father knows what you need before you ask him. Pray then in this way: 'Our Father in heaven, hallowed be your name. Your kingdom come. Your will be done, on earth as it is in heaven. Give us this day our daily bread. And forgive us our debts, as we also have forgiven our debtors. And do not bring us to the time of trial, but rescue us from the evil one.' For if you forgive others their trespasses, your heavenly Father will also forgive you; but if you do not forgive others, neither will your Father forgive your trespasses" (Matthew 6:5-15).

God is constantly speaking to us through nature, through Scripture, and through His many providential interactions. But that is not enough to keep us in a close relationship with Him. We also need to talk to Him. Prayer is opening our hearts to God just as we do with a friend. Prayer doesn't bring God down to us; it lifts us up to Him.

When Jesus lived here on earth, He taught His disciples how to pray. He told them to tell God about their needs and to share with Him their trials and difficulties. Jesus spoke from experience. All that He endured from day to day, surrounded by sin, He shared with His Father. That's how He found comfort and strength to carry on. If Jesus felt that need to pray regularly, constantly, how much more we need to do so as well.[57]

Never be reluctant to pray, for prayer is the key in the hand of faith to unlock heaven's treasure house. Without regular prayer we are in danger of growing careless and losing our way.

Now, there are some conditions on which we can expect God to hear and answer our prayers. To begin, we must feel a need for His help. Unless our hearts are open to the Spirit's influence we can't receive God's blessing. The Bible says, "Ask and it will be given to you; seek and you will find; knock and the door will be opened to you" (Matthew 7:7, NIV).

Next, we need to have faith. Jesus said to His disciples, "Whatever you ask for in prayer, believe that you have received it, and it will be yours" (Mark 11:24, NIV). Even when we do not receive the exact things we pray for, we need to believe; we need to have faith. When it seems our prayers are not being answered, hold on! Believe, trust in the promise, and the answer will come. God is too wise to make a mistake and too good to keep from us anything that is for our best good.[58]

When we come to ask for a blessing from God, we should have a spirit of forgiveness in our heart. Jesus reminds us of this in His model prayer by saying, "Forgive us our debts, as we also have forgiven our debtors" (Matthew 6:12, NIV). If we expect our prayers to be heard, we must forgive others in the same way and to the same extent as we hope to be forgiven.[59]

Daily, continual prayer keeps our lives united with God, so we must never allow anything to interrupt this prayer connection. Pray with others, pray with the family, but, above all, take time for personal, private prayer, for it is the very lifeblood of your soul.[60]

What will you talk to God about in your personal prayers? Everything! Your wants and needs, your happiness and sadness, your problems and fears, tell it all to God. He will never consider a single word or request a burden, no matter how long or how much you pray.

Certainly nothing is too great for Him to notice; remember, He sustains all the worlds of the universe. Nothing is too small for His interest and desire to help you. If it's something of concern to you, it's a concern to Him, too.

Jesus says, "I will do whatever you ask in my name" (John 14:13). To pray in the name of Jesus means more than merely mentioning His name at the beginning or end of a prayer. It means praying in the spirit of Jesus, believing His promises, relying upon His grace, and acting as He would have us act.

God is not asking us to become hermits or monks and retire from the world. He is calling us to live like Jesus, and to alternate between "the mountain of isolation and peace" and the crowds where we live and study and work each day. A person who does nothing but pray will soon stop praying meaningfully.

If we were to talk to God every time He showed His care for us, we would hardly stop talking to Him in prayer all day! We talk about our own lives with our friends because that's where our interests lie. We talk about our friends because we love them. Well, we have an infinitely greater reason to love God than to love our friends, so it should be the most natural thing in the world to make Him first in our thoughts, to talk of His goodness, and to share with others His power in our lives.

Our devotional time should not be only about asking. When we pray, we need to take time to express our thanks for the way God has led and blessed us. God is like a most tender, merciful Father. For that reason, serving Him should never be thought of as a dreary, distressing duty. It needs to become our pleasure and inspiration. In your personal prayer time, think about His cross, His love, His sacrifice, and then you will begin to express your thanks and praise for His magnificent gift for you. You will know that Jesus loves and cares for you, and you can cheerfully go about your daily activities, knowing Jesus expects to go with you as your best Friend.[61]

CHAPTER 8

HOW TO HAVE FAITH

He put before them another parable: "The kingdom of heaven is like a mustard seed that someone took and sowed in his field; it is the smallest of all the seeds, but when it has grown it is the greatest of shrubs and becomes a tree, so that the birds of the air come and make nests in its branches" (Matthew 13:31, 32).

When they came to the crowd, a man came to him, knelt before him, and said, "Lord, have mercy on my son, for he is an epileptic and he suffers terribly; he often falls into the fire and often into the water. And I brought him to your disciples, but they could not cure him." Jesus answered, "You faithless and perverse generation, how much longer must I be with you? How much longer must I put up with you? Bring him here to me" (Matthew 17:14-17).

Everyone wants to have peace of mind. But you know you can't buy it or earn it. What a relief to discover you can have it as a gift! No matter what evils may have been part of your former way of life, as you confess them to Jesus He'll forgive them all, give you a new heart (to use the Bible's metaphor), and let you start all over again. He really does give you a genuine second chance, because that's precisely what He's promised.

While on this earth Jesus taught us that the gifts He promises are ours if we believe. He healed many people of their illnesses and disabilities when they placed their faith in

His power. That help in the physical realm gave them the confidence that they could trust Him for a similar miracle in the spiritual realm.

Do you recall the story of the paralytic at Bethesda? This man was helpless; he hadn't used his limbs for 38 years. Yet Jesus simply told him, "Stand up, take your bed and go to your home" (Matthew 9:6). This poor fellow could have come up with any number of arguments why He couldn't do that, based on 38 years of experience, but he believed Jesus, believed he could walk. He made the decision to try. And the moment he made the decision to be responsive to Jesus' words, God supplied the power! He walked![62]

It's the same with a spiritual miracle. None of us, of ourselves, can do anything about our past sins. We can't change our hearts or make ourselves in the least good. But God promises to do it for us through Jesus. All He asks is that we believe His promise, ask forgiveness for our sins, and commit ourselves to Him. In other words, we make a decision; we use our will. And the moment we believe—believe we are forgiven and cleansed—God supplies the fact. So keep thinking about that paralyzed person. He was healed. And spiritually, the same can happen to us, too, if we believe it.

Don't wait to feel good about your decision. Say to yourself, "I believe it; it's so, because God promised." Then never turn back! From that day you'll be a new person.[63]

You see, once you've given yourself to Jesus in this way and accepted Him as your Savior, He sees you as completely good, no matter how sinful your life may have been. In fact, from that moment Jesus' character stands in place of your character from His point of view. He sees you as if you had never sinned at all. What a gift![64]

As time goes by, you may have to deal with a suspicion

or two that this promise is meant for someone else, but not you. At such a moment God's angels will surround you, bringing God's grace and strength and the reminder that there is no sin He can't forgive if you repent and confess it.[65]

CHAPTER 9

Preparing to Die

He came out and went, as was his custom, to the Mount of Olives; and the disciples followed him. When he reached the place, he said to them, "Pray that you may not come into the time of trial." Then he withdrew from them about a stone's throw, knelt down, and prayed, "Father, if you are willing, remove this cup from me; yet, not my will but yours be done" (Luke 22:39-42).

With His disciples Jesus slowly made His way to Gethsemane. The moon on that Passover evening shone from a cloudless sky. The tents of all the pilgrims who had come to Jerusalem for the feast were silent.

Earlier Jesus had been in intense conversation with His disciples, but as they neared Gethsemane, He became strangely silent. He often came to this place for meditation and prayer, but never before had He come with a heart as troubled as on this night. He seemed to have lost His Father's support as He came to the moment when He would bear the sins of the world. The disciples couldn't help noticing the great change that had come over their Master.

Near the entrance to the garden Jesus left most of the disciples, asking them to pray for Him and for themselves. Then, accompanied by Peter, James, and John, He went further into the garden, where He asked them also to pray. He stumbled on a few more steps, still within their sight and hearing, and collapsed on the ground. As a human being He began to suffer the results of humanity's sin.[66]

Jesus and Satan had met in deadly conflict in the wilderness three years before at the beginning of His earthly ministry, and there He overcame. Now the tempter comes for one final, fearful assault. Everything is at stake for him. If he fails this time, his hope of becoming the master of the world will be gone. In His agony Jesus clings to the cool ground as if to stop Himself from being drawn any farther from the Father, and from His lips comes the cry, "My Father, if it is possible, let this cup pass from me; yet not what I want but what you want" (Matthew 26:39).

Every human being desires sympathy in times of suffering. Jesus longed for sympathy too. In His time of ultimate agony, He came to His disciples for their comfort. He had always supported them in their troubles, and He longed to know they were praying for Him. He staggered over to the place where He had left them, only to find all three of them asleep. Earlier, as Jesus warned them of the coming conflict, they had all assured Him they would willingly face prison or death on His behalf. Peter had added that even if all the rest of them failed, he would not.[67]

With incredible sadness Jesus wakened His sleeping disciples. Addressing Peter, Jesus asked, "Couldn't you support me for just one hour? You are so willing, but also so weak." Sorrowfully, Jesus turned aside to struggle on alone, and there He sweat drops of blood that fell to the ground to mingle with the dew.

"Again he went away for the second time and prayed, 'My Father, if this cannot pass unless I drink it, your will be done'" (Matthew 26:42). The first reaction of the three disciples was to rush to His side, but they concluded they should do what He had asked them to do. So they prayed, then gradually slipped back to sleep. Later Jesus approached them for a second time and found them sleeping. They stirred when He came to them, but they found themselves speechless in His presence. At the sight of His blood-streaked brow they were overwhelmed with fear, unable to understand what was going on.[68]

Returning to His place of anguish, Jesus again prayed for His own tempted, agonized soul. What an awesome moment! The destiny of the world was about to be decided. The future of humanity hung in the balance. Even at this moment Jesus could have declined to take the place of guilty humanity. It was not too late to put this all aside. He could leave the world in its sinfulness and return to His Father in heaven. But again, and then again—yes, three times—He prayed to the Father: "Not my will but yours be done."[69]

Angels were watching Jesus' agony. They saw the legions of satanic forces around Him. Heaven was silent; no music could be played at this profound moment. They watched the Father separating His love from His beloved Son. Unfallen worlds watched with the most intense interest as the conflict on earth drew to its climax.

Some time later, even as Christ's agony continued, His deep depression and discouragement left Him and calmly, with peace written on His bloodstained face, He rose to face Calvary.

As He walked back to the place where all the disciples slept, Jesus was conscious of the approaching mob and woke His associates by announcing the arrival of His betrayer. Standing in front of the disciples, Jesus faced the mob and asked, "Whom do you seek?" When they replied, "Jesus of Nazareth," Jesus answered, "I am He."

As He spoke an angel stood between Him and the mob. A divine light illuminated Jesus' face, and a dovelike form cast its shadow. At that sight the murderous thugs staggered back. Priests, elders, soldiers—even Judas—fell to the ground.

At that moment Jesus could easily have escaped, but He stood His ground even as His accusers lay at His feet. The disciples looked on the scene in silence and awe.

Then the scene quickly changed. As the angel withdrew, its glory fading into the night, soldiers, priests, and Judas stood up and faced Jesus. Ashamed of their weakness and afraid that Jesus might escape, they again said they wanted Jesus of Nazareth, and Jesus answered, "I told you that I am he. So if you are looking for me, let these men go" (John 18:8). That evening He had seen abundant evidence of His friends' weak faith, and He wanted to protect them from further temptation and trial.

"Now the betrayer had given them a sign, saying, 'The one I will kiss is the man; arrest him'" (Matthew 26:48). For a moment Judas pretends he has no association with the mob. Stepping up to Jesus, he takes His hand and says, "Greetings, Rabbi!" and kisses him repeatedly, pretending that he is crying in sympathy with Jesus' peril. But Jesus responds, "Judas, is it with a kiss that you are betraying the Son of Man?" (Luke 22:48). If anything could have, this should have stirred Judas' conscience. Sadly, he remained defiant, showing no sign of repentance for this horrible betrayal.[70]

"Then Jesus said to the chief priests, the officers of the temple police, and the elders who had come for him, 'Have you come out with swords and clubs as if I were a bandit? When I was with you day after day in the temple, you did not lay hands on me. But this is your hour, and the power of darkness!'" (verses 52, 53).

The disciples were terrified as they saw Jesus allow Himself to be taken and bound. They couldn't understand it, and blamed Him for submitting to the mob. In that moment of great fear, Peter proposed that they should save themselves. Following his suggestion, "all the disciples deserted him, and fled" (Matthew 26:56).[71]

CHAPTER 10

CRUEL CRUCIFIXION

When Pilate heard these words, he brought Jesus outside and sat on the judge's bench at a place called The Stone Pavement, or in Hebrew Gabbatha. Now it was the day of Preparation for the Passover; and it was about noon. He said to the Jews, "Here is your King!" They cried out, "Away with him! Away with him! Crucify him!" Pilate asked them, "Shall I crucify your King?" The chief priests answered, "We have no king but the emperor." Then he handed him over to them to be crucified. So they took Jesus; and carrying the cross by himself, he went out to what is called The Place of the Skull, which in Hebrew is called Golgotha. There they crucified him, and with him two others, one on either side, with Jesus between them. Pilate also had an inscription written and put on the cross. It read, "Jesus of Nazareth, the King of the Jews." Many of the Jews read this inscription, because the place where Jesus was crucified was near the city; and it was written in Hebrew, in Latin, and in Greek. Then the chief priests of the Jews said to Pilate, "Do not write, 'The King of the Jews,' but, 'This man said, I am King of the Jews.'" Pilate answered, "What I have written I have written." When the soldiers had crucified Jesus, they took his clothes and divided them into four parts, one for each soldier. They also took his tunic; now the tunic was seamless, woven in one piece from the top. So they said to one another, "Let us not tear it, but cast lots for it to see who will get it." This was to fulfill what the scripture says, "They divided my clothes among themselves, and for my clothing they cast lots." And that is what the soldiers did. Meanwhile, standing near the cross of Jesus were his mother, and his mother's sister, Mary the wife of Clopas, and Mary Magdalene. When Jesus saw his mother and the disciple whom he loved standing beside her, he said to his mother, "Woman, here is your son." Then he said to the disciple, "Here is your mother." And from that hour the disciple took her into his own home. After this, when Jesus knew that all was now finished, he said (in order to fulfill the scripture), "I am thirsty." A jar full of sour wine was standing there. So they put a sponge full of the wine on a branch of hyssop and held it to his mouth. When Jesus had received the wine, he said, "It is finished." Then he bowed his head and gave up his spirit (John 19:13-30).

As news of Jesus' fate spread through Jerusalem, a vast crowd gathered and followed Him along the way to Calvary. When He passed the gate into Pilate's court, they placed on His bruised and bleeding shoulder the cross that had been intended for Barabbas. But the weight of a cross was more than Jesus could carry. He hadn't eaten since the Passover supper with His disciples on Thursday evening. Then He had battled with Satan in Gethsemane, suffered the betrayal of Judas, watched His disciples desert Him and flee, stood before Annas, Caiaphas, Pilate, and Herod, and twice endured lashes on His back. When they put the cross on His shoulder, He collapsed. It was more than any human being could bear.

Mary, in the company of John, saw her Son collapse. She longed to take His wounded head in her hands and wipe the brow that had once rested on her breast. But she could not.

At that moment a Cyrenian, Simon, arriving from the country, found himself surrounded by the crowd. He heard the mocking cry, "Make way for the King of the Jews!" Amazed at the unbelievable cruelty and hostility, he stopped to express compassion for Jesus. The soldiers seized him, placed Jesus' cross on his shoulders, and forced him to carry it all the way to Calvary. For the rest of his life Simon looked back on that event as a privilege that led him to take up the cross of Christ from choice.

The women in the crowd watched the developments with intense interest. Some of them had seen Jesus when they'd brought loved ones to Him for healing. They were astounded at the hatred displayed by the angry mob, for their own hearts were breaking in sympathy for Him. As Jesus fell fainting beneath the cross, the women gasped and cried out in empathy. Their mournful wails were all that Jesus noticed as He staggered along. Despite His intense suffering as He carried the sins of the world, He looked up at these women with compassion. They were not His disciples. They weren't crying for Him as God's Son, but they openly showed their feelings of pity for Him. Jesus noticed. Though He appreciated their sympathy, His greater concern was for their future. Where would they be for eternity?

Arriving at the place of execution, the three prisoners were bound to their torture stakes. Both thieves resisted and had to be wrestled onto their crosses, but Jesus offered no resistance. Mary, supported by John, watched, hoping that somehow Jesus would demonstrate His power and free Himself. At the same time His words describing the very scene she now witnessed came into her mind.

Mary's mind swirled with many questions. Would her Son, who had raised the dead, allow Himself to be crucified? Would she have to give up her belief in His Messiahship? Was there no way for her to reach out and give Him some comfort? She watched each step in the cruel process until she saw the soldiers take His hands and drive spikes through them. At that she fainted and had to be carried away.

Through the entire ordeal Jesus never spoke a word of complaint. He breathed only this compassionate prayer: "Father, forgive them; for they do not know what they are doing" (Luke 23:34). The prayer He offered that day included every person in the world, from creation to the end of time. We all bear guilt for the crucifixion of Jesus, but Jesus offers us forgiveness so we can experience peace now and claim His promise of eternal life.

After the soldiers had nailed Jesus to His cross they lifted it up and dropped it violently into place. This caused Jesus the most intense physical agony. They nailed a sign above His head that read, in Hebrew, Greek, and Latin: "Jesus of Nazareth the King of the Jews." Providentially, through that sign thousands of visitors from the surrounding countries who had come to Jerusalem for the Passover feast heard for the first time the truth about Jesus.[72]

In a small gesture of humaneness, Romans soldiers were permitted to give a drug to the victims of crucifixion to diminish some of their excruciating pain. When they offered it to Jesus, however, He tasted it and refused it. He would not allow His mind to be dulled in this way. His mind must remain clear to find strength to hold on to God through faith.

Ridicule continued as the day wore on. The religious leaders joined the mob in mocking Jesus with cruel taunts: "If you are the Son of God, come down from the cross." "He saved others; he cannot save himself" (Matthew 27:40, 42). Their taunts contained a cruel truth—Jesus could have taken Himself down from the cross, but had He done so and saved Himself, He could not have saved sinners.

Throughout His agony, Jesus found comfort in one brief conversation, initiated by a request from the repentant thief beside Him. When the soldiers bound the thieves to their crosses, both of them had ridiculed Jesus, but as the hours passed, a change came over one of them. This man was no hardened criminal. Earlier in his life he had seen Jesus' ministry and had been convicted by what he heard. But those convictions were diminished by the accusations of the priests.

Led on by a poor choice of friends, he immersed himself in a life of sin that ended in his arrest, trial, and sentence to die.

While most people in the crowd at Calvary ridiculed Jesus, there were some who heard and recalled His words and deeds of compassion and quietly defended Him. As the thief heard these people talk, it reawakened his earlier convictions. Turning to the other thief, he asked, "Don't you fear God, seeing you're suffering the same fate?" The dying thieves had nothing more to fear from human beings, but what about God and the judgment? The repentant thief moaned that they were receiving the results of their criminal lives, but looking at Jesus, he exclaimed: "This man has done nothing wrong" (Luke 23:41).

The more the thief thought about it, the more his doubts began to evaporate. He recalled all he had heard about Jesus, remembered those He had healed, those whose sins He had forgiven. He glanced at Jesus' friends weeping below him, read the sign above Jesus' head, and, little by little, the Holy Spirit brought the chain of evidence together. He recognized in Jesus the Lamb of God that takes away the sin of the world. In a strange mixture of hope and fear, the thief reached out to Jesus and begged, "Lord, remember me when You come into Your kingdom" (verse 42, NKJV). Instantly he heard this astounding assurance: "You will be with me in paradise" (verse 43).

As Jesus also looked over the crowd below Him, He noticed His mother and John. Sensing the end for Jesus was near, John had brought her back to the cross. As He approached death, Jesus thought of the needs of His mother. Looking into her grief-stricken face, and then at John, He said to her, "This is your son." Then to John He charged, "This is your mother!" John fully understood the significance of those words, and he took Mary to his home, where he cared for her for the rest of her life.

While carrying the awful weight of the guilt of the world, Jesus was deprived of His Father's presence. That terrible deprivation in His time of ultimate anguish pierced His heart with a sadness that no human being can comprehend. The pain of the separation from His Father eclipsed even His extraordinary physical pain. During those lonely hours Jesus feared that sin was so offensive to His Father that They would be separated forever. In the end that sense of the Father's intense anger over the sins of the world that Jesus carried as our Substitute broke His heart. In this experience Jesus felt the same anguish every unrepentant sinner will feel at the end of time when God's mercy has been withdrawn from the world.

Even the sun refused to witness this tragic scene. At midday darkness enveloped the cross for about three hours. In the eerie darkness lightning occasionally flashed, illuminating the cross and the Crucified. In these strange and unexplained demonstrations of nature, religious leaders, executioners, and the milling crowd imagined that their time of punishment for what they had done had come. Then about 3:00 they heard Jesus cry out, "My God, my God, why have you forsaken me?" (Matthew 27:46).

Visualize the scene. The sinless Son of God hangs, dying, on a cross. His back is shredded from being lashed twice. His hands that had continuously reached out to bless others are nailed to the wooden bars. His feet that had walked tirelessly on missions of love are also nailed. His royal brow is punctured by the thorns that form a mocking crown. And He suffers it all without the sustaining presence of His Father. Never forget that it is for you that Jesus agreed to bear this unbelievable burden of guilt! He died to open the gates of Paradise for you!

Late on that blood-soaked Friday afternoon a voice is heard from the central cross. In perfect clarity that all at

Calvary could hear, Jesus announced, "It is finished" (John 29:30). He added, "Father, into Your hands I commit My spirit" (Luke 23:46, NKJV). At that moment a strong light circled the cross, and Jesus' face shone as bright as the sun. Then His head dropped . . . and He died.[73]

CHAPTER 11

GRAND RESURRECTION

Early on the first day of the week, while it was still dark, Mary Magdalene came to the tomb and saw that the stone had been removed from the tomb. So she ran and went to Simon Peter and the other disciple, the one whom Jesus loved, and said to them, "They have taken the Lord out of the tomb, and we do not know where they have laid him." Then Peter and the other disciple set out and went toward the tomb. The two were running together, but the other disciple outran Peter and reached the tomb first. He bent down to look in and saw the linen wrappings lying there, but he did not go in.

Then Simon Peter came, following him, and went into the tomb. He saw the linen wrappings lying there, and the cloth that had been on Jesus' head, not lying with the linen wrappings but rolled up in a place by itself. Then the other disciple, who reached the tomb first, also went in, and he saw and believed; for as yet they did not understand the scripture, that he must rise from the dead. Then the disciples returned to their homes. But Mary stood weeping outside the tomb.

As she wept, she bent over to look into the tomb; and she saw two angels in white, sitting where the body of Jesus had been lying, one at the head and the other at the feet. They said to her, "Woman, why are you weeping?" She said to them, "They have taken away my Lord, and I do not know where they have laid him." When she had said this, she turned around and saw Jesus standing there, but she did not know that it was Jesus.

Jesus said to her, "Woman, why are you weeping? Whom are you looking for?" Supposing him to be the gardener, she said to him, "Sir, if you have carried him away, tell me where you have laid him, and I will take him away." Jesus said to her, "Mary!" She turned and said to him in Hebrew, "Rabbouni!" (which means Teacher). Jesus said to her, "Do not hold on to me, because I have not yet ascended to the Father. But go to my brothers and say to them, 'I am ascending to my Father and your Father, to my God and your God'" (John 20:1-17).

The hours of Saturday night passed silently until the darkest time of all, just before dawn. And all the while, Jesus lay as a prisoner of death in the grave. The great stone stood firmly in its place, the Roman seal remained unbroken, and the Roman guards continued on duty. Suddenly a great earthquake shook the land at the approach of an angel from heaven, surrounded by God's glory. All the soldiers fell to the ground as if they were dead.

The guards saw Rome's official seal to the tomb shattered as the angel rolled away the heavy stone as if it were a pebble. Then they heard the angel speak at the entrance to the cave: "Son of God, come out! Your Father calls You." Immediately Jesus rose, walked out of the grave, and proclaimed, "I am the resurrection and the life."

Through the reeling of the earth, the flashing of lightning, and the roaring of thunder, the eyes of the soldiers remained riveted on Christ's radiant face. Was this the One they had seen standing as an unresisting prisoner in the judgment hall before Pilate and Herod? the One for whom they'd made a crown of thorns? the One whose back had been lacerated with a scourge? the One they had nailed to the cross? the One they had mocked? the One the priests taunted, wagging their heads as they said, "He saved others; he cannot save himself" (Matthew 27:42)?[74]

Now in awe and fear, they knew that nothing could hold Him prisoner of death. If they had piled mountains upon mountains over His grave, He would still have come out alive!

As the glory of the angels vanished in the first glimmerings of dawn, the soldiers struggled to their feet, stumbling like drunks, and headed into Jerusalem, telling the news to everyone they met. As they were making their way to Pilate, the report came to the Jewish authorities, and the chief priests sent for the soldiers to be brought to them first.

Still trembling from the events at the grave, their faces still colorless, the Roman guards testified convincingly that Jesus had been raised from the dead. They told the whole story exactly as they had witnessed it. There had been no time or motivation to speak anything but the truth. As the priests listened, their faces went deathly pale. Caiaphas tried to speak. His lips moved, but no sound came. Ultimately, as the soldiers turned to leave, Caiphas found his voice and said, "Wait! Don't tell anyone what you saw."

Then the priests made up a lie for the soldiers. "Report that His disciples came during the night and stole His body while you were asleep." What an unbelievable lie! If the soldiers were asleep when the disciples stole the body, how could they have known? And if the disciples had stolen His body, surely the priests would be the first to condemn them! The soldiers were horrified at the thought of bringing upon themselves the charge of sleeping on duty. That was a crime for which they could pay with their lives. To pacify the soldiers, the priests promised them protection and hush money if they followed their instructions.[75]

Back at the garden tomb very early that Sunday morning the women who had stood at the cross made their way to the tomb, carrying spices to anoint Jesus' body. The thought that He might have risen from the dead didn't enter their minds. As they approached the garden, they asked each other who would roll away the great stone that blocked the entrance. They knew they couldn't. Then they felt the earth begin to tremble beneath their feet and saw the sky illuminate with glory. When they reached the tomb, the stone already had been moved, and they found no body inside.

Mary Magdalene, who had reached the tomb first, wasted no time in running to tell the disciples. Moments later, when the other women arrived, they sensed they were not alone. Looking around, they saw someone sitting by the tomb. It was the angel who had rolled away the stone.

The brightness surrounding the angel frightened them, and they turned to leave. The angel's words stopped them in their tracks. "Don't be afraid; I know you are looking for Jesus. He isn't here! He's alive! Come and look at the place where His body rested. Then go quickly, and tell His disciples."

Only then did the women recall His words about rising from the dead, and they realized they had no need of the expensive anointing spices they had brought.

Mary, not having heard the news of Jesus' resurrection, reached Peter and John before the other women and shared the shocking news that someone had taken the body of Jesus. So the three of them ran back to the tomb and confirmed what Mary had told them. They saw the shroud there, but no Jesus.

When Peter and John left the tomb and returned to Jerusalem, Mary lingered behind, overwhelmed with grief and wondering who could tell her what had happened to Jesus' body. In the midst of this perplexity, her eyes filled with tears, she heard a voice asking, "Why are you weeping? Who are you looking for?" (John 20:15).[76]

Through her tears Mary could see a figure and presumed it to be the gardener. She asked, "If you took the body away, tell me where you put it." Mary feared the gardener might have thought that this rich man's grave was too honorable a place for someone crucified as a criminal. If that were the case, she would find an appropriate place. Her mind went immediately to the tomb where she and her sister had buried Lazarus before Jesus raised him from the dead.

Then Jesus addressed her again, this time by her name. "Mary!"

She knew instantly this was not the gardener—it was the resurrected Jesus! For a moment she forgot He'd been crucified, and rushed to embrace His feet, exclaiming, "Master!"

Jesus raised His hand and said, "Not now. I must ascend to My Father. Go to My disciples and tell them I am going to My Father, your Father; My God, your God."

Mary left quickly to share this incredible message.[77]

As long as Jesus lay in the grave, Satan hoped that Jesus would not take up His life again. On Friday afternoon Satan claimed the Lord's body and set his own angels to guard the tomb. He felt bitterly angry when the angel from heaven arrived on Sunday morning and scared away his angels! As Satan watched Jesus step out of the grave alive, he knew that his kingdom was doomed and that he would ultimately die.

The priests became the tools of Satan when they arranged for Jesus to be put to death, and on Sunday morning they were still entirely in his power. When they heard the report of the resurrection, they were afraid of the reaction of the people and felt that their own lives were in danger. Their only hope was to try to cast Jesus as an impostor and to deny His resurrection. So they bribed the soldiers, secured Pilate's silence, and spread their lies as far as they could.

However, there were some witnesses they could not silence. Many people had heard the soldiers' startling report on their way into the city. Also, there were others who had been raised from the dead at the same time that Jesus rose. Then Jesus Himself appeared to some, confirming that He was alive. Thus, from that day on, it was the greatest dread of the priests that they themselves might sometime encounter Jesus face to face.

Just as Jesus' words about His death had been fulfilled, so now were His words about His resurrection. He had told His disciples, "I lay down my life, in order to take it up again. . . . I have power to lay it down, and I have power to take it up again." And to the priests He had said, "Destroy this temple, and in three days I will raise it up" (John 10:17, 18; 2:19).

Outside the broken tomb of Joseph of Arimathea Jesus had stated in triumph, "I am the resurrection, and the life." Only God could speak such words. All creatures live by the will and power of God who made them. We are all dependents; we are all recipients of life from God. Only He could honestly say, "I have power to lay down My life, and I have power to take it again." In His divinity Jesus had demonstrated His power to break the shackles of death.

At His resurrection Jesus raised a great number of people who had died. These were people who had worked for God and had given their lives to speak the truth about Him. The earthquake at the time of Jesus' death had broken open those graves, and when Jesus arose, they rose too. During His ministry Jesus had raised the dead on more than one occasion. He raised the son of the widow of Nain, the ruler's daughter, and Lazarus. But none of them were raised to live forever. In time each of them died again. The people who came to life at the time of Jesus' resurrection, however, rose to immortality and ascended with Jesus at His ascension as trophies of His victory over death and the grave.

To the believer, Jesus is both resurrection and life. He said, "I am come that they might have life, and . . . have it more abundantly" (John 10:10, KJV). In Him everything that has been lost through sin will be restored. Life is in Him, and He will bring back to life everyone who chooses Him as Savior. In fact, the moment we accept Jesus, we have everlasting life.

Referring to the Lord's Supper, He said, "Those who eat my flesh and drink my blood have eternal life, and I will raise them up on the last day" (John 6:54). To the Christian death is a sleep, a time of rest. All Jesus' friends are safe in His care, and when He returns they will be with Him in His glory forever.

At the last day the voice of Jesus will be heard from heaven. It will penetrate graves and open them, and those who "sleep in Jesus" will rise to life. At His own resurrection only a few graves were opened, but at His second coming all His sleeping friends will hear His voice, and rise to life and immortality.[78]

The promise of Jesus' second coming remained fresh in the minds of the disciples all their lives. They knew that the same Jesus they had watched ascending into heaven would return. The same voice that had said "I am with you always, to the end of the age" (Matthew 28:20) would one day welcome them into the kingdom of heaven.[79]

The disciples now understood the work they had been commissioned to do. They knew they must share the truths Jesus had taught them. They must tell the story of Jesus life, death, and resurrection, the mysteries of salvation, and the power of God to forgive sins. Through the Holy Spirit's power they would share these themes everywhere.[80]

CHAPTER 12

How to Handle Doubts and Confusion

Never be anxious about whether or not you are saved. By making yourself the center of that question your thoughts become centered on yourself and away from Jesus. Once you've committed your life to Him, trust Him, talk to Him, think about Him. Put every doubt and fear out of your mind. Here's how.

Young adults, especially, find themselves plagued by doubts. It has many causes. For example, they can't understand some things in the Bible and wonder if they'll ever understand. They may seem unable to get beyond those doubts. Here's something to hold on to: God never asks a person to believe anything without giving enough evidence on which to base one's faith. His existence, His character, the truthfulness of the Bible all can be accepted by the reasonable evidence He provides. God doesn't remove the possibility of doubt, for He wants us to have faith. Anyone who wants to doubt can find reasons to do so. Likewise, all who really want to know what is true will find plenty of evidence on which to rest their faith.

Our minds are finite, and it is impossible for us to comprehend what is infinite. The most brilliant mind, the most educated person, will always face the ultimate mystery in the study of God. God's Word has many mysteries we'll never understand: how sin came into the world, how Jesus came to earth as a man, how He was raised from the dead, how we are saved. These are all mysteries beyond our full understanding. But that's no reason to disbelieve them! We can't understand life in the physical world, even the simplest forms, so should we be surprised to find mysteries in the spiritual world that we can't fathom?

Skeptics love to argue that the many things in Scripture we can't understand are a good argument against accepting it as God's Word. But you can argue just as compellingly that its mysteries are the most persuasive argument for its divine origin. And, paradoxically, it shows us the way to be saved with a simplicity that anyone who chooses to understand can understand. The more we search the Bible, the deeper will be our conviction that these are honestly the words of God.

We all come to the Bible with a certain amount of pride, and it's humbling to realize that we are face to face with some things we can't understand no matter how hard we study. It's God's plan that the truths of His Word will constantly become clearer to us as we read them. Here's how that happens. He has given us His Spirit to guide our thoughts as we read the Bible. Shortly before His crucifixion, He told His disciples that He would send them the Spirit to guide them in their knowledge of truth. He said, "When the Spirit of truth comes, he will guide you into all the truth. . . . He will take from what is mine and declare it to you" (John 16:13, 14). Your understanding begins as you study the Word, led by the Spirit, utilizing your God-given powers of reason and understanding. So open the book reverently; it is God's Word. Pray for the Spirit's guidance, and you will find yourself moving away from doubts.

But what if, despite all this, doubt continues to haunt you? Then it would be appropriate to ask yourself if your growing knowledge and understanding of God's will is interfering with something you like to do but have begun to realize is not part of God's will for you. If that proves to be true, make the decision that your relationship with Jesus is more important than any part of your former way of life. The Bible has this invitation: "Taste and see that the Lord is good" (Psalm 34:8). So keep "tasting" and find the blessing. Remember Jesus' words: "Ask and you will receive" (John 16:24). Jesus wants you to be happy!

As you pass from death to life you will be able to say, "I needed help, and I found it in Jesus. He has met my soul's hunger, and now the Bible reveals Jesus to me." By faith we may imagine eternity and grasp the promise of God for increased intellect as the Holy Spirit possesses our humanity. Soon everything that has perplexed us in the providences of God will be made plain. As Paul wrote to the church in Corinth: "Now we see in a mirror, dimly, but then we will see face to face. Now I know only in part; then I will know fully, even as I have been fully known" (1 Corinthians 13:12).[81]

(For additional reading on this subject, we recommend *The Desire of Ages, Steps to Christ, The Story of Redemption,* and *The Acts of the Apostles.*)

Think About It

1. Why does God want to save us?
2. For whom was Jesus' first miracle performed?
3. Why did the prodigal's father place his own coat around his son's shoulders?
4. Matthew and the rich young ruler both received invitations to follow Jesus. In what ways were their circumstances similar? In what ways were they different? Why do you think Matthew accepted Jesus' invitation and the rich young ruler did not?
5. What can we learn about effective teaching from the story of the farmer planting seeds? How only can we "bear fruit"?
6. What are some of the conditions to answered prayer?
7. What is the basis of our forgiveness from God?

JUST JESUS IN YOUR LIFE

CHAPTER 13

RELATIONSHIPS

A YOUNG ADULT'S ENCOUNTER WITH ELLEN WHITE . . . ON RELATIONSHIPS

I was involved in a relationship that was not right. Some things are "gray issues," but there are times we really do know that something is wrong. I had the "definitely wrong" conviction about my recent relationship with my boyfriend. Yes, he was a Christian, and I even had some friends who told me we were good for each other. But deep down I knew that this was not where God was leading me.

There were other clues, too, such as the fact that the people closest to me—my family and longtime friends—didn't approve. They were impressed (as I was but didn't admit to them) that it was not God's plan for me to be in this relationship. Foolishly, I listened to those who told me what I wanted to hear because this was what I wanted. I didn't leave God. I kept praying and tricking myself into thinking this was His will, even though I knew it wasn't, because I thought this was "true love."

During this same time I was taking a marriage and family psychology class at one of our Seventh-day Adventist universities. Two of the books the professor used were The Adventist Home *and* Messages to Young People. *This was my first time reading these books all the way through. With each page I turned, I was convicted of the truth that I already knew. I was forced to look beyond our dating relationship and all the mushy romantic stuff that I loved to what really mattered. Was this relationship to God's glory? No. I could answer that quite easily.*

I'll be honest. I never intended it to go the way it did. You know how easy it is once you're "in love" with someone to let your physical relationship go farther than you want it to go.

I swore I would never do that. Even if you don't have sex, you very easily can go beyond what is pure and holy when you are together. Ellen White knew this. That's why, as I read her messages, my conscience was pricked. She didn't skip words that needed to be said, such as "Don't be sneaky," "Don't ignore your parents' counsel," "Don't be immodest, impure, or immoral," and "Out of control."

I may have scoffed before or thought that I was somehow "stronger" than temptation, but ultimately I found myself in sin. God told me once again through Mrs. White that my physical relationship had gone too far. Through her He also told me that He loves me still and wants to help me start over.

The writings that God gave to His prophet will never be outdated, even if they seem difficult to follow through on or, at times, even impractical. I know from experience that it's hard to actually carry out God's guidelines, but He offers us strength. It's easy to read those promises—or even say them—but when you are right there in the relationship, what do you do? You read something, you're convicted, and then what?

Even though I messed up so many times, the thing that brought me to victory in this relationship (having it end) was listening, and then making a choice. One practical principle I gleaned by reading Ellen White's counsel on relationships is Don't stay alone together at night. It's easy to rationalize, but eventually God spoke to me through Ellen White and through His Word about things that needed to happen to bring this relationship under His control.

No matter what society does, the wisdom about honoring God in our relationships by practicing purity is always applicable. Ellen White's counsel on relationships helped me finally see that.

—Stephanie, age 21

A Young Adult's Encounter With Ellen White . . . on Relationships

It was my junior year in college when the love of my life told me that he no longer cared for me. My heart broke. I was certain no one had ever hurt as I did, and no one ever would again. I was still ill from a recent hospitalization and struggling with grades and career choice. God seemed far away.

One night, in total discouragement, I sat at my desk, ready to cry, when my hand, resting on my throat, felt the steady pulse of my heart. Instantly a favorite quote from Ellen White came to mind: "Every breath, every pulsation of the heart, is an evidence of the all-pervading care of Him in whom 'we live and move and have our being'" (Acts 17:28).[82]

For a moment I sat in awe, feeling my pulse and hearing "I love you, I love you, I love you" whispered beneath my fingers from the God of the universe, knowing I was loved.

My sweetheart didn't come back, and I still struggled with my health, but I knew, overwhelmingly, that at least I did not face these things alone.

—Anne, age 30

A Young Adult's Encounter With Ellen White . . . on Relationships

Ever since I was 12 I have had the opposite gender on my mind, spending hours talking with my friends about who I was infatuated with at the moment. Until I started reading Ellen White, however, I did not fully realize what a high ideal God has for dating and marriage. I read Messages to Young People *when a friend recommended it to me, and realized how inadequate was my view of a romantic relationship. A marriage and family class in high school required me to read Ellen White's principles for relationships and cemented my desire to follow God's plan for dating standards.*

As a result, I am extremely thankful to God for the messages

He gave Ellen White that have helped me make moral choices that bring peace, not regret.

Ellen White has especially influenced my relationships throughout college as I gave my future love life to God. I am now seriously dating the most wonderful man, and Letters to Young Lovers *has been invaluable to me in evaluating our relationship. As Ellen White intimates, I can look back and see God choosing for me, and leading my boyfriend and me closer to Him and to each other. We have been encouraged greatly by Mrs. White's suggestions, definitely finding in God a sure counselor, and in our parents wonderful confidants and advisors.*

I am reading ideas in Ellen White's books about what a woman should look for in a husband and the true love that God promises to weave in our hearts, and I am finding that God is fulfilling His Word more and more in my life. I praise God for speaking to me through Ellen White's words of wisdom about relationships. I am finding exquisite joy in following where He leads.

—Rahel, age 23

A Young Adult's Encounter With Ellen White . . . on Relationships

I am indebted to God for His messages to me through for His holy Word and Mrs. White's writings, and to my family for their counsel in the area of romantic relationships. In Patriarchs and Prophets, *in the chapter titled "The Marriage of Isaac," Mrs. White lays out the principle that has led to so much joy and fulfillment in my own relationship. That principle? Isaac believed God Himself would direct in the choice of his wife-to-be. His simple trust is my inspiration and my model.*

In my early years of dating I would have been wiser to follow Isaac's example of trust in his parents regarding his future spouse. However, my parents' prayers for me paid off when God used my mistakes to bring me to the realization that I must leave my relationship hopes and dreams completely in His hands.

God is teaching me through His biblical principles and in Mrs. White's writings concerning the matter of my future wife and the importance of both of us being totally committed to Him. Because of our unconditional commitment to Him, and our faith that God Himself is directing all our choices, my girlfriend and I relish searching together for relationship principles, in both the Bible and in Ellen White's writings. The trust we're learning as we see God's providence and direction has allowed us to experience increasing joy in the freedom and purity of His holy law.

Ellen White's writings have been an invaluable guiding light in the formation of my "philosophy of relationships."

—Kirk, age 23

Scripture

Love is patient; love is kind; love is not envious or boastful or arrogant or rude. It does not insist on its own way; it is not irritable or resentful; it does not rejoice in wrongdoing, but rejoices in the truth. It bears all things, believes all things, hopes all things, endures all things. Love never ends. But as for prophecies, they will come to an end; as for tongues, they will cease; as for knowledge, it will come to an end (1 Corinthians 13:4-8).

He who finds a wife finds a good thing, and obtains favor from the Lord (Proverbs 18:22).

Do not be mismatched with unbelievers. For what partnership is there between righteousness and lawlessness? Or what fellowship is there between light and darkness? (2 Corinthians 6:14).

For this is the will of God, your sanctification: that you abstain from fornication; that each one of you know how to control your own body in holiness and honor, not with lustful passion, like the Gentiles who do not know God. . . . For God did not call us to impurity but in holiness (1 Thessalonians 4:3-7).

Let us live honorably as in the day, not in reveling and drunkenness, not in debauchery and licentiousness, not in quarreling and jealousy. Instead, put on the Lord Jesus Christ, and make no pro-

vision for the flesh, to gratify its desires (Romans 13:13, 14).

Blessed are the pure in heart, for they will see God (Matthew 5:8).

For your maker is your husband, the Lord of hosts is his name; the Holy One of Israel is your Redeemer (Isaiah 54:5).

So the ransomed of the Lord shall return, and come to Zion with singing; everlasting joy shall be upon their heads; they shall obtain joy and gladness, and sorrow and sighing shall flee away (Isaiah 51:11).

Ellen G. White letter 51, 1894

Norfolk Villa, Prospect Street
Granville, New South Wales, Australia
August 9, 1894

Dear Nellie:

I am thankful to God that you love the truth and that you love Jesus. I am anxious that you should press your way forward and upward in order that you shall reach the standard of Christian character that is revealed in the Word of God. Let the Word of God be your guidebook that in everything you may be molded in conduct and character according to its requirements.

You are the Lord's property; He created you and He redeemed you. You may be a light in your home and a positive influence. When the truth of God is in the heart, its saving influence will be felt by everyone in the house. You have a sacred responsibility, one that requires you to keep your soul pure by consecrating yourself to be wholly the Lord's.

Your friends who are totally opposed to spiritual things are not under the leadership of Christ but under the black banner of the prince of darkness. To associate with those who neither respect nor love God—unless you associate with them for the purpose of winning them to Jesus—will be a detriment to your spirituality. If you cannot change their attitudes, their influence will corrupt and taint your own faith. It's good to be kind to these persons, but not good for you to continually try to be with them and do the things they do; for if you choose the atmosphere that surrounds them, you will forfeit the companionship of Jesus.

From the light that the Lord has given, I warn you that you are in danger of being deceived by the enemy. You are in danger of choosing your own way and of not following the counsel of God and not walking in obedience to His will. The Holy One has given rules for the guidance of every person so that no one need miss their way. These directions mean everything to us, for they form the standard to which every son and daughter of Adam should conform.

You are just entering upon womanhood, and if you seek Jesus, you will grow in grace, become wiser by experience, and as you advance from light to greater light you will become happier. Remember your life belongs to Jesus, and that you are not to live for yourself alone.

Shun those who are irreverent. Shun one who is lazy; shun the one who scoffs about sacred things. Avoid becoming close friends with those who use profanity or who are addicted to even one glass of alcohol. Don't fall for the proposals of a man who has no realization of his responsibility to God. The pure truth which sets you apart for a holy purpose will give you courage to cut yourself loose from even a handsome, caring man whom you know does not love and respect God and knows nothing about the principles of true rightdoing. We should always be patient with a friend's failings and with his ignorance, but never with his degrading habits.

Be cautious every step that you take; you need Jesus at every step. Your life is too precious to be treated as of little worth. Calvary testifies to you of your value. Consult the Word of God in order to know how you should live your life that was purchased for you at such immense cost. As a child of God you are permitted to marry only in the Lord.

Be sure that you do not follow your own heart alone, but make choices based on your respect for God.

If believers associate with unbelievers for the purpose of winning them to Christ, they will witness for Christ, and then withdraw in order to breathe again in a pure and holy atmosphere. When you are with unbelievers, remember that you are a representative of Jesus Christ; don't speak shallow and superficial words or participate in cheap conversation. Keep in mind the value of every person. Remember that it is your privilege and your duty to be working together with God in every possible way. You are not to lower yourself to the same level as that of unbelievers, and joke and laugh at crude or vulgar conversation.

The Lord will help you and, if you trust Him, will bring you up to a high standard. Through the grace of Christ you can make right use of your spiritual gifts and become an agent for good in winning persons to Jesus. Every talent you have should be used on the right side.

My dear young friend, I have written to you because I love you, and I urge you to hear my words. I have more to write to you when I can find time.

With Christian love,
Ellen White[83]

ELLEN G. WHITE LETTER 23, 1886

Great Grimsby, England
September 23, 1886

Dear Rolf:

While at Basel I had some conversations with Edith in regard to your attentions to her. I asked her if she were sure she loves you well enough to marry you. She answered that she wasn't quite certain. I told her she should really know what she was doing, that she should give no encouragement to the attentions of any young man, showing him preference, unless she loved him. . . .

I told her she should consider the goal of a marriage with you, whether by such a step you could both glorify God, whether you would be more spiritual, and whether your lives would be more useful. Marriages that are impulsive and selfishly planned generally do not result well, but often turn out miserable failures.

I had reason to think that she doesn't enjoy household tasks, and I knew you should have a wife who could make your home happy. I asked her if she had any experience in household management. I asked her these questions because it had been presented to me that she needed special education in practical duties of life, but that she really had no interest in those things.

Now, Rolf, I cannot say that it is my business to say that you should not marry Edith, but I will say that I have an interest in you. Here are things that should be considered: Will the one you marry bring happiness to your home? Is Edith financially stable, or will she, if married, not only use up all her own earnings but all of yours to gratify vanity, a love of appearance? Are her principles correct on this subject?

I do not think Edith knows what self-denial is. If she had the opportunity she would find ways to spend even more money than she has done. With her, selfish spending has never been overcome, and this natural self-indulgence has become a part of her life. She desires an easy, fun time.

I must speak plainly. I know, Rolf, that should you marry her you would be mated but not matched. There would be something missing in the one you make your life partner. And as far as Christian devotion and spiritual life is concerned, that can never grow where so great selfishness possesses the soul.

I am writing to you, Rolf, just as I would write to my

son. There is a great and important work lying just before us, and the part we will act in this world depends wholly upon our aims and purposes in life. We may be following impulse. You have the qualities in you to make you a useful man, but if you follow inclination, this strong current of stubbornness will sweep you away. Set a high goal and focus on reaching it.

Let your ruling purpose be to grow to a complete man in Christ Jesus. In Christ you can have courage to make a difference; without Christ you can do nothing as you should. You have a determination to achieve your goals. This is not an objectionable feature in your character if all your powers are surrendered to God. Please, think about this: you don't have the freedom to be an impulsive lover. Christ has purchased you with a price that is infinite. You are His property, and in all your plans you must take this into your thinking.

Especially in your marriage planning, be careful to get a partner who will stand shoulder to shoulder with you in spiritual growth.

Rolf, I want you to consider all these things. God help you to pray over this matter. Angels are watching this struggle. I leave you with these things to consider and decide for yourself.

Ellen White[84]

(For additional reading on this subject, we recommend *Messages to Young People, Letters to Young Lovers,* and *The Adventist Home.)*

Think About It

1. What two or three basic human needs are satisfied by a Christian marriage relationship?

2. Identify several biblical principles that should lead in the choice of a life companion.

3. What do you think it means to be "mated, but not matched"? (See p. 77.)

4. How will the commitment to sexual purity before marriage increase personal happiness afterward?

CHAPTER 14

WELLNESS

A YOUNG ADULT'S ENCOUNTER WITH ELLEN WHITE . . . ON WELLNESS

There is much focus on health these days. You've seen it—many diets, gyms, and health foods. Men and women are trying to get in shape. Complicated programs are everywhere, but I have seen that being healthy is actually quite simple. I don't mean that using all your willpower to resist that piece of chocolate cake is easy, but the principles behind the whole thing are. I know there are people with special health needs, but for most of us what we eat and what we do determine how fit we are.

I had been a vegetarian for more than three years when I started my first year of college. I also started reading The Ministry of Healing, *and discovered it was really interesting. That book sounds just like what the health community is currently publishing! Where I live there is a great focus on health, but it seemed ironic for me to be reading a book about health that had been written more than 100 years ago and yet contains the same basic guidelines as the modern journals.*

I started following the vegan lifestyle and increased my exercise, intake of water, and time with God. Within the first semester, I was not only feeling better physically (and minus those excess 25 pounds), but more connected spiritually. When I resisted my appetite, I found that I was stronger against temptation. Also, since my brain was no longer clouded from a high-sugar, high-fat diet I discovered that I could hear the voice of God more clearly.

Ellen White's counsel made a visible, tangible difference in my health and appearance. More important, practicing that counsel has strengthened my relationship with my Savior

—Tara, age 21

A Young Adult's Encounter With Ellen White . . . on Wellness

I grew up vegetarian, but still didn't always make healthy choices. Although my family always ate healthfully, I grabbed at any chance I could get to sneak in desserts and snacks. However, I took a class on Daniel in academy and was required to read Ellen White's counsels on diet, rest, exercise, and health, in order to better understand Daniel's example.

I began to realize that even though I was a vegetarian I wasn't living up to the information I knew about healthful living. I cut out dairy products, refined foods, and most sugar. I soon felt like a new person and could remember what I studied much better. I also began a regular exercise program, tried to get more sleep, and drank more water. I am still continually astonished at how seldom I get sick, how much more energy I have, and how much more efficiently I study in comparison to the previous years of my life.

Another aspect of mental wellness that Ellen White has brought to my attention is trusting in God. I am a chronic worrier, and doubts and fears used to dominate my thoughts and prayers. However, God continues to change my heart slowly and imperceptibly, often through Ellen White's writings. She reminds me that my trust is in the Omnipotent One, who longs to give me peace and wants me to know how much He cares about every detail of my life. One of my favorite quotes is from In Heavenly Places: *"Educate yourself to have unlimited confidence in God."*[85] *I long to do that day by day, and throughout my whole life, as the most integral part of my wellness.*

—Rel, age 21

A Young Adult's Encounter With Ellen White . . . on Wellness

I have worked as a counselor or boys' director at a Seventh-day Adventist youth camp for the past four summers. I am continually searching for the perfect materials to use in my worship thoughts with campers each night. The Bible and Ellen White's writings have been my staples. I use those same writings extensively for wisdom in discipline, my personal meditation, and to answer questions from boys of varying ages.

In this past summer's search for ideal devotional material, my thoughts turned to Ellen White's work The Sanctified Life, *specifically her stories about Daniel and his Hebrew friends in Babylon. I now have adopted the Genesis 1:29 diet and place a high priority on whole, unrefined foods, very little sugar, plenty of sleep, and water. Because these decisions have been so beneficial in the physical, mental, emotional, and spiritual realms of my life, I wanted to share with my campers the inspiration for, and potential benefits of, such changes.*

Each week I would demonstrate my health habits to my campers by declining to eat fried, sugary, or otherwise unhealthy foods in lieu of fruits, vegetables, and grains. "My" boys knew the value I placed on sleep, water, hygiene, and healthy habits through my constant interaction with them and by observing my lifestyle choices. This led them to badger me with questions concerning the health benefits or liabilities of a variety of foods and habits of their own. In turn, our worship thoughts on Daniel and his friends allowed me to share the biblical principles behind my actions and choices. Ellen White's writings on these matters have opened my mind to the benefits of wellness, and I have been privileged to pass on the wealth!

—Brian, age 23

Scripture

Then the king commanded his palace master Ashpenaz to bring some of the Israelites of the royal family and of the nobility, young men without physical defect and handsome, versed in every branch of wisdom, endowed with knowledge and insight, and competent to serve in the king's palace; they were to be taught the literature and language of the Chaldeans. The king assigned them a daily portion of the royal rations of food and wine. They were to be educated for three years, so that at the end of that time they could be stationed in the king's court. Among them were Daniel, Hananiah, Mishael, and Azariah, from the tribe of Judah. The palace master gave them other names: Daniel he called Belteshazzar, Hananiah he called Shadrach, Mishael he called Meshach, and Azariah he called Abednego.

But Daniel resolved that he would not defile himself with the royal rations of food and wine; so he asked the palace master to allow him not to defile himself. Now God allowed Daniel to receive favor and compassion from the palace master. The palace master said to Daniel, "I am afraid of my lord the king; he has appointed your food and your drink. If he should see you in poorer condition than the other young men of your own age, you would endanger my head with the king" (Daniel 1:3-10).

"Please test your servants for ten days. Let us be given vegetables to eat and water to drink. You can then compare our appearance with the appearance of the young men who eat the royal rations, and deal with your servants according to what you observe."

So he agreed to this proposal and tested them for ten days. At the end of ten days it was observed that they appeared better and fatter than all the young men who had been eating the royal rations. So the guard continued to withdraw their royal rations and the wine they were to drink, and gave them vegetables. To these four young men God gave knowledge and skill in every aspect of literature and wisdom; Daniel also had insight into all visions and dreams.

At the end of the time that the king had set for them to be brought in, the palace master brought them into the presence of Nebuchadnezzar, and the king spoke with them. And among them all, no one was found to compare with Daniel, Hananiah, Mishael, and Azariah; therefore they were stationed in the king's court. In every matter of wisdom and understanding concerning which the king inquired of them, he found them ten times better than all the magicians and enchanters in his whole kingdom (verses 12-20).

Beloved, I pray that all may go well with you and that you may be in good health, just as it is well with your soul (2 John 2).

Do you not know that your body is a temple of the Holy Spirit, who is in you, whom you have received from God? You are not your own; you were bought at a price. Therefore honor God with your body (1 Corinthians 6:19, 20, NIV).

So, whether you eat or drink, or whatever you do, do everything for the glory of God (1 Corinthians 10:31).

Among the Israelites who were taken as prisoners of war to Babylon were men and women who were as true as steel to principle, not corrupted by selfishness but willing to honor God at the loss of everything. In the land of their captivity these individuals were to carry out God's purpose by showing to non-Christian nations the benefits that come through knowing God. They were to be His representatives. Never were they to compromise their faith. In good times and bad they honored God, and God honored them.

Daniel and his three friends stood up for God—wonderful examples of what young people may become when they unite with the God of wisdom and power. From the comparative simplicity of their Jewish homes, these youth from royalty were taken to the most fabulous of cities and directly into the court of the world's greatest emperor.

Seeing enormous intellectual potential in these young men, Nebuchadnezzar decided that they should be trained to fill important positions in his kingdom. To prepare them for their administrative careers, he arranged Chaldean language study, as well as entrance to the three-year specialized education reserved for royalty.

A crucial test came right at the beginning of their elite

training. As a token of the king's approval and personal interest in their welfare, he provided the Jewish students with cuisine and drinks from his own table. However, since part of the meal had been offered to idols, anyone who ate it would be recognized as respecting the gods of Babylon. Loyalty to Jehovah prohibited Daniel and his friends from honoring a false god in any way. Even pretending to eat the food or drink the wine would be denying their faith.

Additionally, these young people dared not risk reducing their vitality and squandering their physical, mental, and spiritual health. They remembered the sad results of Nadab and Abihu's drinking, and didn't want to injure their own physical and mental powers through the use of wine.

Daniel and his friends had come from homes in which parents had emphasized abstinence from alcohol. They had been taught that God would hold them accountable for their talents and abilities, and they must never undermine or deplete their strength. This early childhood education helped Daniel and his friends make good choices, though degrading influences and strong temptations were all around them in the luxurious and corrupt court. No power, no influence, could move them from the principles they had learned earlier by studying the Word and works of God.

If Daniel had desired, he certainly could have found an excuse in his surroundings for giving up his strictly temperate habits. He could have argued that since he was dependent on the king's approval and subject to his power, there was no other option for him than to eat from the king's food and drink his wine. If he followed God's teaching, he would offend the king and probably lose his position, and even his life. On the other hand, if he ignored the commandment of the Lord, he could keep the approval of the king and guarantee a highly successful career.

But Daniel did not hesitate. The approval of God was

more important to him than the approval of the most powerful earthly monarch, more important than life itself. Whatever the outcome, he would stand firm. He "resolved that he would not defile himself with the royal rations of food and wine" (verse 8). His three friends supported his position.

The Hebrew youth were not arrogant in coming to this decision. They relied totally on God. They didn't go out of their way to be odd, but if being peculiar was necessary in order to honor God, they were willing. If they yielded to wrong in this situation because of the pressure of circumstances, that compromise would weaken their sense of right and their hatred of wrong. The first wrong step would lead to others until their connection with heaven would be cut off, and they would be swept away by temptation.[86]

Daniel appealed to Melzar, the officer in special charge of the Hebrew youth, requesting that they might be excused from eating the king's food and drinking his wine. He asked for a ten-day trial of simple food, while the other captives ate royal gourmet.

Melzar, though worried that going along with this request would bring on the displeasure of the king, nevertheless consented. Daniel knew that his case was won! Sure enough, at the end of the ten days' trial the outcome was exactly opposite of what the officer feared. In personal appearance the Hebrew youth were much more fit and strong than their other friends. As a result, Daniel and his associates were permitted to continue their simple diet during their entire course of training.

For three years the Hebrew youth concentrated on Chaldean studies. During this time they remained loyal to God and depended constantly on His power. Along with practicing self-discipline, they combined goal setting with focus and hard work. It was not pride or ambition that brought them into the king's court, into fraternity with those who didn't know or respect God; they were prisoners of war in a foreign country, placed there by Eternal Wisdom. Separated from home influences and spiritually minded friends, they tried to conduct themselves with distinction for the honor of their oppressed homeland and for the honor of Him whom they served.

The Lord approved the firmness, altruism, and pure motives of the Hebrew youth and gave them His blessings. He gave knowledge and skill in every aspect of literature and wisdom; Daniel also had insight into all visions and dreams (verse 17). The promise was fulfilled: "Those who honor me I will honor" (1 Samuel 2:30). As Daniel clung to God with unwavering trust, the spirit of prophetic power came upon him. During the time that Daniel was learning the duties of court life from his teachers, God was teaching him to read the mysteries of the future and to record events covering the history of this world until the close of time.

At the examinations at the end of the training period, the Hebrews were tested for placement in government service. But "among them all, no one was found to compare with Daniel, Hananiah, Mishael, and Azariah" (Daniel 1:19). Their keen comprehension, their extensive knowledge, their precise and articulate language, testified to the unimpaired strength and vigor of their mental ability. "In every matter of wisdom and understanding concerning which the king inquired of them, he found them ten times better than all the magicians and enchanters in his whole kingdom" (verse 20).

Brilliant students, representing every country, the most talented, highly intelligent, and culturally educated youth in the world, could not compare with the young Hebrews. Strongest, most handsome, most knowledgeable, and with the quickest recall—they stood at the top, living testimonials of healthful living.

Though far more successful in the examinations than

their fellow students, Daniel and his friends' academic success did not come from chance. They did well because of the disciplined use of their abilities, under the guidance of the Holy Spirit. They chose to connect with the Source of all wisdom, making the knowledge of God the foundation of their education. In faith, they prayed for wisdom, and they lived their prayers. They placed themselves where God could bless them, avoiding anything that would weaken their abilities and taking advantage of every opportunity to learn in all subject areas. They followed the rules of health, guaranteeing strength of intellect. They pursued knowledge for one purpose: that they might honor God. And God Himself was their teacher. Constantly praying, conscientiously studying, keeping in touch with the Unseen, they walked with God, as did Enoch.[87]

Through the consistent practice of health principles demonstrated by the Hebrew youth, God is speaking to the youth of today. Where are young men and young women who, like Daniel, will do and dare for the cause of right? Pure hearts, strong hands, fearless courage are needed. The warfare between good and evil calls for constant watchfulness. Satan comes to every person with temptation in many alluring forms to indulge appetite.

The body is the most important agency through which the mind and the soul are developed for building character. That is why the adversary, Satan, directs his temptations toward weakening and degrading physical power. If he succeeds here, it often means the surrender of the whole being to evil. The tendencies of our physical nature, unless under the control of a higher power, will eventually bring ruin and death. The body must be disciplined. Our passions must be controlled by choices submitted to God's will. Consecrated reason is king! Intellectual power, physical stamina, and length of life depend upon unchangeable laws. Through obedience to these laws of health, youth may conquer themselves, conquer their own inclinations, and conquer the "rulers of the darkness of this world" (Ephesians 6:12, KJV).

The spirit of Daniel can be the spirit of the youth today; they may draw from the same source of strength, possess the same power of self-control, and reveal the same grace in their lives, even under similarly unfavorable circumstances. Though surrounded by temptations to indulge self, especially in our large cities, where every form of sensual gratification is made easy and inviting, youth may resist every temptation. But only to those who determine to do right because it is right will the victory be gained.

God desires to reveal through you today the same mighty truths that were revealed through these young men. The life of Daniel and his friends is a demonstration of what He will do for you if you seek Him with your whole heart.[88]

(For additional reading on this subject, we recommend *The Ministry of Healing, Counsels on Diet and Foods, Counsels on Health,* and *Temperance.*)

Think About It

1. What are several advantages of healthful eating to the serious Christian?
2. What three things might you change in your lifestyle that could result in more peace in your life?
3. Identify several reasons Daniel and the three worthies did not eat Nebuchadenezzar's food.
4. Think of several examples of life issues in which it is appropriate to "dare to be a Daniel." Where might it be better to compromise?
5. What is the relationship between appetite, self-control, and Christian character?

CHAPTER 15

SOCIAL JUSTICE

A YOUNG ADULT'S ENCOUNTER WITH ELLEN WHITE . . . ON SOCIAL JUSTICE

I never thought a lot about Ellen G. White. I knew she existed and was highly regarded within our church. I had read a few required readings here and there during my school years, but I never really paid much attention to any of it until I found the following passage: "Our Lord Jesus Christ came to this world as the unwearied servant of man's necessity. . . . He came to give [men] health and peace. . . . None who came to Him went away unhelped. . . . The Saviour's work was not restricted to any time or place. His compassion knew no limit. . . . Wherever there were hearts ready to receive His message, He comforted them with the assurance of their heavenly Father's love. . . . His life was one of constant self-sacrifice. . . . Jesus devoted more time to healing the sick than to preaching."[89]

Two years ago I started to work online with teens in crisis. Some are pregnant and unmarried and don't know where to turn; some are in abusive homes or relationships. But all of them are looking for someone to care, someone to let them know that it will be OK in the end. And what better person to show that than Christ? And what better place to read about how He helped people than in the book The Ministry of Healing*?*

The principles from the chapter "Helping the Tempted" are so relevant to my work. I cannot help these kids by pointing out their mistakes to them. I can't preach at them and tell them what they did wrong and throw them back out on the street. They need someone to reassure them that someone still loves them and that they still matter. And after reading The Ministry of Healing, *by Ellen G. White, I have learned through Christ's example, as explained in the book, to go about that in a better way.*

—Jodi, age 21

Scripture

Is not this the fast that I choose: to loose the bonds of injustice, to undo the thongs of the yoke, to let the oppressed go free, and to break every yoke? Is it not to share your bread with the hungry, and bring the homeless poor into your house; when you see the naked, to cover them, and not to hide yourself from your own kin? Then your light shall break forth like the dawn, and your healing shall spring up quickly; your vindicator shall go before you (Isaiah 58:6-8).

When the Son of Man comes in his glory, and all the angels with him, then he will sit on the throne of his glory. All the nations will be gathered before him, and he will separate people one from another as a shepherd separates the sheep from the goats, and he will put the sheep at his right hand and the goats at the left.

Then the king will say to those at his right hand, "Come, you that are blessed by my Father, inherit the kingdom prepared for you from the foundation of the world; for I was hungry and you gave me food, I was thirsty and you gave me something to drink, I was a stranger and you welcomed me, I was naked and you gave me clothing, I was sick and you took care of me, I was in prison and you visited me."

Then the righteous will answer him, "Lord, when was it that we saw you hungry and gave you food, or thirsty and gave you something to drink? And when was it that we saw you a stranger and welcomed you, or naked and gave you clothing? And when was it that we saw you sick or in prison and visited you?" And the king will answer them, "Truly I tell you, just as you did it to one of the least of these who are members of my family, you did it to me."

Then he will say to those at his left hand, "You that are accursed, depart from me into the eternal fire prepared for the devil and his angels; for I was hungry and you gave me no food, I was thirsty and you gave me nothing to drink, I was a stranger and you did not welcome me, naked and you did not give me clothing, sick and in prison and you did not visit me." Then they also will answer, "Lord, when was it that we saw you hungry or thirsty or a stranger or naked or sick or in prison, and did not take care of you?" Then he will answer them, "Truly I tell you, just as you did not do it to one of the least of these, you did not do it to me." And these will go away into eternal punishment, but the righteous into eternal life" (Matthew 25:31-46).

Happy are those who consider the poor; the Lord delivers them in the day of trouble (Psalm 41:1).

Give justice to the weak and the orphan; maintain the right of the lowly and the destitute. Rescue the weak and the needy; deliver them from the hand of the wicked (Psalm 82:3, 4).

Those who oppress the poor insult their Maker, but those who are kind to the needy honor him (Proverbs 14:31).

Whoever is kind to the poor lends to the Lord, and will be repaid in full (Proverbs 19:17).

In Matthew 25 Jesus identifies Himself with His suffering people. Jesus is hungry and thirsty. Jesus is the stranger. Jesus needs clothes. Jesus is sick. Jesus is in prison. When you are enjoying a wide variety of delicious food, Jesus is famishing in farm worker housing not far from you.

Jesus says, "When you closed your door in My face, while your beautifully decorated rooms were unoccupied, I had no place to lay My head. When your closets were filled with trendy and expensive outfits, purchased with money that could have helped the needy, I had no comfortable clothes. When you were enjoying health, I was sick. While you roamed free, misfortune cast Me into prison, disillusioned Me and stigmatized Me, depriving Me of freedom and hope."

What solidarity Jesus expresses between Himself and His suffering children! He makes their case His own. Their misery is His misery. Take note, selfish Christian: Each neglect of the needy poor, the homeless, the fatherless, the prisoner, is neglect of Jesus.[90]

When you doled out the small pittance of bread to the starving poor, when you gave those flimsy garments to shield them from the biting frost, did you remember that you were giving to the Lord of glory? "All the days of your life I was near you in the person of these afflicted ones, but you did not seek Me. You would not consider friendship with Me. I know you not."[91]

The poor have as much right to a place in God's world as have the wealthy. The principles from the book of Leviticus are given by our merciful Creator to lessen suffering, to bring hope and sunshine into the lives of the destitute and oppressed.

The Lord says Stop! to the inordinate love of property and power. Great evil results from the continued accumulation of wealth by one class and the poverty and degradation of another. Without some restraint the power of the wealthy becomes a monopoly, and the poor, though in every way fully as worthy in God's sight, are considered and treated as inferior to the more prosperous. The sense of this oppression arouses the passions of the poorer class. There is a feeling of despair and desperation that demoralizes society and opens the door to crimes of every description. The regulations God established in Leviticus were designed to promote social equality.[92]

God's Word prohibits policies that will enrich one class of persons through the oppression and suffering of another class. The person who takes advantage of someone's misfortunes for monetary benefit, or who seeks a profit through another's weakness or incompetence, breaks the law of God.[93] Society abandons the poor to misery and degradation, not caring that many have been brought to the depths of poverty by illness or misfortune, often through the dishonest scheming of those who live by preying upon the less fortunate.[94]

There are entire communities in which families live in substandard housing, with little furniture and clothing, without books or equipment for work, destitute both of comforts and conveniences and means of culture. These families must be educated to the potential for improvement. How can this be done where poverty is prevalent, where long-held habits and attitudes of defeat must be met at every step? Certainly, this work is difficult. The necessary reformation will never be made unless men and women are assisted by a power outside themselves. While helping the poor in temporal things, always keep in view their spiritual needs.[95] It is God's purpose that the rich and the poor shall be closely bound together by the ties of sympathy and usefulness. Those who have money, talent, and ability are to use these gifts in benefiting humanity.[96]

Real charity helps men and women to help themselves. If someone asks you for food, you should not turn that person away. True philanthropy means more than mere gifts. It means a genuine interest in the welfare of others. We should try to understand the needs and environment of the poor and distressed and give them the help that will benefit them most. To give thought and time and personal effort costs far more than merely giving money. But it is the truest charity.[97]

Often, the most effective way to help the poor is to offer education in practical lines, providing opportunities for job placement training, cooking classes, and personal finance. Those who are taught to earn what they receive will more readily apply fiscal responsibility. In learning to be self-reliant, they are also empowered and equipped to help others.

Many persons who struggle financially would benefit from learning economic management. Teach the importance of living up to the potential Christ gives to each person.[98]

Jesus sought to correct the world's false standard of judging the value of men and women. He took His position with the poor that He might lift the stigma from them. He has stripped the prejudice from poverty by blessing the poor and inviting them to inherit His kingdom. He points us to the same path He walked, saying, "If any want to become my followers, let them deny themselves and take up their cross daily and follow me" (Luke 9:23).[99]

We are all woven together in the great web of humanity, and whatever we can do to benefit and uplift others will reflect blessings back to us. The law of mutual dependence runs through all classes of society.[100]

Each of you can find something to do for the less fortunate. "You always have the poor with you," Jesus said (John 12:8). Each of you can find opportunities to help. Millions and millions of human beings, ready to perish, bound in chains of ignorance and sin, have never heard that Jesus loves them. What if their condition was ours, and ours were theirs? What would we want them to do for us? The answer to that question is what we are obligated to do for others. Christ's rule of life, by which every one of us must stand or fall in the judgment, is: "In everything do to others as you would have them do to you" (Matthew 7:12).[101]

(For additional reading on this subject we recommend *Gospel Workers*, *The Ministry of Healing*, and *Welfare Ministry*.)

Think About It

Identify several things we can do for young adults who are abused and hurting.

1. How did Jesus suggest we could help those with special needs? (See Matthew 25:31-46.)
2. Briefly characterize several principles of "real charity."
3. If you were poor and destitute, what would you want most from others? Rank your three most desirable choices.
4. In "that great judgment day," what will Christ present before the nations as the basis of our salvation?

CHAPTER 16

CAREERS

A YOUNG ADULT'S ENCOUNTER WITH ELLEN WHITE . . . ON CAREERS

Ellen White counseled that every well-educated woman should know how to harness a horse. How could a Victorian woman, who lived at the turn of the twentieth century, help me choose a career at the turn of the twenty-first century? Computer programmer, radiology technician, helicopter pilot, substance abuse counselor—many of my job options didn't even exist in her lifetime!

Even though Ellen White was not familiar with twenty-first-century technology, she helped me understand the cosmic significance of life. My life matters to God. He wants me to be with Him in heaven. He needs me to choose to do His work on earth.

Based on the advice and counsel of Ellen White, I determined that my mission—career, if you please—was to be a minister of the gospel in everything I did. When people asked me what my college major was, I'd reply, "I'm a ministry student! More than studying about God, I want to learn how to work with, and for, Him!"

So far God has employed me as a dormitory resident assistant, colporteur, youth pastor, and registered nurse. I have continually asked myself, "How can I do this job to make an eternal difference for me or someone else?" Only God knows what work I will do in the future; but through Ellen White I have this career assurance: "Not more surely is the place prepared for us in the heavenly man-

sions than is the special place designated on earth where we are to work for God."[102]

—Julie, age 24

Young Adult's Encounter With Ellen White . . . on Careers

In elementary school my ambition was to be a player on a professional basketball, football, or baseball team. As time went on, I realized that that goal was a dream and not reality.

When, as a teenager, I began to realize how much God loves me as an individual, I wanted to know Him as a personal friend. I tried to read spiritual books, but found them boring. A couple years later I again picked up Steps to Christ. *And this time it came alive. God began speaking directly to my heart, and I wanted to share how much Jesus means to me.*

I believe that God used Ellen White to inspire me to grow in a love relationship with Christ and to commit my career to Him. I realized that working to save people for Jesus' kingdom means that God could help me to trust Him and love Him more deeply.

Right now I am a student gospel literature evangelist, but I want to be a witness, no matter what line of work I ultimately choose. Only doing something to help others will truly make me happy. I don't want to get caught up in the rat race, because the love of money will lead me to hell.

Reading about Jesus in The Desire of Ages *has helped me decide to dedicate my life to ministry and evangelism.*

I read a Help Wanted sign into Luke 10:2: "The harvest truly is great, but the laborers are few; therefore pray the Lord of the harvest to send out laborers into His harvest" (NKJV). God is urgently calling young people to work for Him today! I choose to go and gather precious persons for God's harvest.

—Tim, age 21

SCRIPTURE

Trust in the Lord with all your heart, and do not rely on your own insight. In all your ways acknowledge him, and he will make straight your paths. Do not be wise in your own eyes; fear the Lord, and turn away from evil (Proverbs 3:5-7).

For surely I know the plans I have for you, says the Lord, plans for your welfare and not for harm, to give you a future with hope (Jeremiah 29:11).

But strive first for the kingdom of God and his righteousness, and all these things will be given to you as well (Matthew 6:33).

For what will it profit them if they gain the whole world but forfeit their life? (Matthew 16:26).

Go therefore and make disciples of all nations, baptizing them in the name of the Father and of the Son and of the Holy Spirit, and teaching them to obey everything that I have commanded you. And remember, I am with you always, to the end of the age (Matthew 28:19, 20).

And this good news of the kingdom will be proclaimed throughout the world, as a testimony to all the nations; and then the end will come (Matthew 24:14).

Dear youth, what is the aim and purpose of your life? Are you ambitious for education that will give you prestige and honor? Do you have dreams you can't even express—that you will one day stand upon the summit of intellectual greatness? Do you hope to one day sit as a legislator and help enact laws for the nation? There is nothing wrong in these aspirations. Each of you can reach your goals. Don't be content with mediocrity. Aim high, and exert yourself to reach your goal.[103]

Success in any line demands a definite aim. If you want to achieve true success in life, set goals worthy of your efforts. The highest purpose for your life is to give the gospel to the world in this generation. That purpose opens opportunities for everyone whose heart Jesus has touched.

God's purpose for you is wider, deeper, higher than your limited vision has ever imagined! God often picks reliable persons from unlikely places to witness for Him in the world's highest places. Many a young person of today, growing up like Daniel in his Judean home, studying God's Word and His works, and learning lessons of responsibility, will yet stand in legislative assemblies, in courtrooms, and before royalty, as a witness for the King of kings.[104]

True education does not ignore the value of scientific knowledge or literary attainments; but above information it values power; above power, goodness; above intellectual achievements, character. The world does not so much need persons of great intellect as of great character. The world needs young men and young women whose talents are controlled by consistent principles.[105]

What, then, is essential education for this time? True education embraces physical, mental, and moral training that develops all your abilities to their highest potential so you can serve God and work to benefit humanity. To seek for fame and recognition will separate you from the Spirit of God, depriving you of that grace which would make your work for Christ effective.[106]

Students who exalt the sciences above the God of science will be ignorant, even though they think they are brilliant. If you cannot afford time to pray, cannot take time to communicate with God and reflect on the Source of wisdom, your learning will be wasted.[107]

God's career choice for us is determined by our capabilities. Not everyone has the same ability. Regardless of your academic potential, each of you should aim just as high as uniting yourself with divine power allows you to reach.[108]

Love and loyalty to Jesus are the spring of all real service. When your heart is touched by Christ's love, you will want to work for Him. Look for ways to serve the poor, the victimized, and the oppressed. Like any other work, skill comes as you actually become involved in ministry and service to the disadavantaged. Without actual involvement and exposure to their needs, even well-meaning efforts can have disastrous results. After all, you learn to swim in the water, not on land!

The church is organized for service, and in a life of service for Jesus connection with the church is one of the first steps. Loyalty to Christ demands responsibly carrying out church duties. This is an important part of your education, and in a church that reflects Jesus' life it will lead directly to helping a world in pain.

There are many ways youth can find opportunities for service to others. Organize yourselves into small groups and look for ways to serve the community. Working together will give you a sense of unity, acceptance, and encouragement. Parents and teachers can be your mentors, and you will benefit from the wisdom of their experience.

Learn about others' needs! That knowledge kindles empathy, which is the basis for effective ministry. As you try to learn about the tremendous needs of persons in developing countries, you will become less self-centered and more sympathetic to the desperate plight of millions. Find out all you can about persons such as the apostle Paul, Martin Luther, Moffat, Livingston, and Carey, as well as today's frontier missionaries.

God alone knows the depths of the world's misery and despair, and He knows how to bring relief. Everywhere He sees hurting persons, crushed with sin and sorrow and pain. But He also sees their potential; He sees the height that they could reach. Although human beings have abused their opportunities, wasted their talents, and lost their Godlike dignity, the Creator will be honored in their rescue.[109]

Thousands of young persons will be called to this rescue

ministry. The whole world is opening to the gospel. From every direction sin-stricken hearts cry for a knowledge of the God of love. Millions have never heard of God or of His love. It is their right to receive this knowledge. They have equal rights to the Savior's mercy. We must answer their cry. At this crisis, the question asked of Queen Esther comes to every home, every school, every student who has enjoyed the light of the gospel: "Who knows whether you have come to the kingdom for such a time as this?" (Esther 4:14, NKJV).

There is no line of work that could benefit you more than helping the underprivileged. In this ministry, you are God's helping hand. Through you, angels can carry out their mission. Angels can speak through your voice and work through your hands. As you cooperate with these heavenly beings you receive the benefit of their education and experience. What university course could equal this?

With such an army of workers as our youth, rightly trained, might furnish, how soon the message of a crucified, risen and soon-coming Savior might be carried to the whole world! How soon might the end come—the end of suffering and sorrow and sin! How soon, in place of our lives here, marred by sin and pain, we could inherit heaven, where the voice of weeping will never again be heard.[110]

All the perplexities of our life's experience we will then understand. What appeared to be only confusion, disappointment, and frustration will be seen as God's beautiful plan to give us victory at last. There we will again meet our friends. The love and caring that God planted in our hearts will have true and sweet fulfillment. Visiting with God, enjoying life with the angels and with God's friends from all history, experiencing the special bonds of unity—these are among the joys of heaven.

In our life here, earthly, sin-restricted as it is, the greatest joy and highest education are in service. And in the future reality, uninhibited by the limitations of sinful humanity, we will find our greatest joy and highest education in service—witnessing and learning rich mysteries: Christ in you, the hope of glory.[111]

(For additional reading on this subject we recommend *True Education; Counsels to Parents, Teachers, and Students; Colporteur Ministry; Fundamentals of Christian Education;* and *Christian Service.*)

Think About It

1. What is the relationship between choice of career and choice of a ministry for God?
2. Is it wrong to be ambitious? Why, or why not?
3. What personal values are associated with "true education"?
4. How can one "cooperate with God and heavenly angels" for the good of others?
5. What is "true service" for others?

CHAPTER 17

AUTHORITY OF SCRIPTURE

A YOUNG ADULT'S ENCOUNTER WITH ELLEN WHITE . . . ON THE AUTHORITY OF SCRIPTURE

To put it simply, one of the main reasons I believe in Ellen White is that she never puts her writings above the Bible. Think about it: There are churches and denominations today whose teachings and beliefs depend on their founder or prophet, not on the Bible. That's not the way it is in the Seventh-day Adventist Church. Ellen White always made it clear that she was the lesser light leading to the greater light of God's Word. I can see in her writings that she was only seeking to bring people to God and did not want to lift herself up above the Bible or call attention to herself.

Jesus says, "And I, if I be lifted up from the earth, will draw all men unto me" (John 12:32, KJV). This is what I see Ellen White doing. She lifts up Jesus and His Word. I believe God sent Ellen White as a prophet to our church. Right now, as you well know, not everyone my age believes in the message of Ellen White to modern-day Christians. I would even venture to guess that the majority of young adults don't read or believe.

I've been there. I questioned why the writings of this woman from 100 years ago even fit into our lives today. The reason I can say so definitely that Ellen White has value as a modern-day prophet is that I see her (1) lifting up Jesus, and (2) upholding the Bible as the Word of God and the final authority for Christians. The true testimony is that by reading her books people fall in love with Jesus, and that leads them to reading more in the Word of God.

I know that is true, because it happened to me.

—Jo, age 21

A Young Adult's Encounter With Ellen White . . . on the Authority of Scripture

The quality of Ellen White that draws me to her most is her love of Jesus and her insistence on the authority of Scripture. Many times she has expressed in her writings that Scripture alone is the basis for the truth. She considered herself a "lesser light to lead men and women to the greater light [the Bible]."[112]

These statements give me confidence that I can trust her writings in my daily walk with God. I thank the Lord for the fabulous asset of Mrs. White's writings that have been given to help us better understand biblical truths. She was a messenger for the Lord, and she understood that role and abided by it with utmost faithfulness and responsibility. I respect her for that and use her writings as another tool in my study of Scripture. Nothing can replace the Bible, and I am very sensitive to the thought of someone criticizing or trying to change the Bible. I take assurance in knowing that Mrs. White felt that same way. When I read Patriarchs and Prophets *or* The Great Controversy, *the Bible comes alive for me!*

As far as I'm concerned, the Bible is my guidebook on the journey of my life, and Mrs. White's writings are somewhat like the Cliff Notes.

—Michael, age 26

Scripture

From childhood you have known the sacred writings that are able to instruct you for salvation through faith in Christ Jesus. All scripture is inspired by God and is useful for teaching, for reproof, for correction, and for training in righteousness, so that everyone who belongs to God may be proficient, equipped for every good work (2 Timothy 3:15-17).

You search the scriptures because you think that in them you have eternal life; and it is they that testify on my behalf (John 5:39).

I warn everyone who hears the words of the prophecy of this book: if anyone adds to them, God will add to that person the plagues described in this book; if anyone takes away from the words of the book of this prophecy, God will take away that person's share in the tree of life and in the holy city, which are described in this book (Revelation 22:18, 19).

Now if people say to you, "Consult the ghosts and the familiar spirits that chirp and mutter; should not a people consult their gods, the dead on behalf of the living, for teaching and for instruction?" (Isaiah 8:19, 20).

These Jews were more receptive than those in Thessalonica, for they welcomed the message very eagerly and examined the scriptures every day to see whether these things were so (Acts 17:11).

The Bible is more valuable as an educating power than the writings of all the philosophers of all ages. With a wide range of style and subjects, the Bible has something interesting and morally instructive for everyone. The light of revelation shines brightly into the distant past, where chronicles of history fail to illuminate. Biblical poetry evokes the wonder and admiration of the world. In glowing beauty, in sublime and solemn majesty, in touching pathos, it is unequaled by the most brilliant productions of human genius. The Bible contains sound logic and impassioned eloquence. It portrays courageous acts of integrity, examples of private goodness and public honor, lessons of holiness and purity.[113]

Nothing will energize the mind and strengthen the intellect more than the study of the Word of God. No other book has the power to uplift thoughts and invigorate abilities as the Bible. If God's Word were studied as it should be, men and women would have the open mind, excellent character, and firm purpose that are rarely seen in these times. The search for truth will reward the seeker, and each discovery will open up more valuable fields for investigation.[114]

We should prize the Bible because it reveals the will of God. Here we learn the object for our creation and how to attain that objective. We learn how to make wise use of the present life and how to obtain the future life. No other book can satisfy the questionings of the mind or the cravings of the heart. As we acquire a knowledge of God's Word and practice it in our lives, we may rise from the lowest depths of degradation to become children of God, the companions of sinless angels.[115]

In searching the Scriptures, in reflecting on the words of life, consider it as the voice of God to the soul. We may be confused sometimes over the voice of our friends; but in the Bible we have the counsel of God upon all important subjects which concern our eternal interests. Even in our secular affairs we may learn a great deal from the Bible. Its teaching will be always suited to our individual circumstances, preparing us to endure trial and making us ready for our God-given work.

The Bible is God's voice speaking to us, just as surely as if we could hear it with our ears. If we realized this, we would open God's Word with awe and seriously search its laws. Reading and contemplating the Scriptures would be considered as an audience with the Eternal God.[116]

What book can compare with the Bible? An understanding of its teachings is essential for every child and youth, as well as older persons, for it is the word of God, given to guide the human family to heaven. In the world today many things are idolized, and there are many philosophies and ideologies. Without an understanding of the Scriptures it is impossible for the youth to understand what is truth, or to tell the difference between the sacred and the ordinary.[117]

The people of God must look to the Scriptures as their safety against the influence of false teachers and the deceiving power of the spirits of darkness. Satan tries everything possible to prevent everyone from knowing the Bible, because its plain teachings reveal his deceptions. Whenever God's work revives, the prince of evil rises to more intense activity. Right now Satan is exerting his strongest efforts for a final struggle against Jesus and His followers. The last great deception is just ready to open to our view. The antichrist will perform miracles that we will actually see. The counterfeit will be so similar to the true that the only way to know the difference will be by the Bible. By the principles of Scripture every statement and miracle must be tested.

Those who are trying to obey all the commandments of God will be opposed and mocked. We can stand only in God. In order to stand up to the trial ahead of us, we must understand God's will as revealed in His Word. We can honor God only as we understand his character, government, and purposes. Only those who have strengthened their minds with the truths of the Bible will stand through the last great conflict. To each of us will come the searching test: Will I obey God rather than human beings? That decisive hour is right upon us. Are our feet planted on the rock of God's unchanging word? Are we prepared to stand firm in defense of the commandments of God and the faith of Jesus?

When God sends warnings so important that they are symbolized by holy angels flying through the heavens, He requires each of us to pay attention. The awful judgments against the worship of the beast and his image (Revelation 14:9–11) should lead all of us to a diligent study of the prophecies to find out what the mark of the beast is and how we can avoid receiving it. But the masses of the people turn away from hearing the truth and turn toward fables and mysticism. The apostle Paul declared, looking down to the last days, "The time will come when they will not endure sound doctrine" (2 Timothy 4:3, KJV). That time is here. Most people do not want Bible truth because it interferes with the desires of their sinful, world-loving hearts. Satan then supplies the deceptions that they love.

But God will have a group of people on the earth who maintain the Bible, and the Bible only, as the standard for all doctrines and the basis of all reforms. The opinions of educated men and women, the deductions of science, the many conflicting creeds or decisions of religious organizations, the voice of the majority—none of these things should be the basis for or against any point of religious faith. Instead, before accepting any teaching or doctrine, we should demand a plain "This is what God says" in its support.

Satan is constantly trying to attract attention to humans in the place of God. He leads people to look to bishops, to pastors, to professors of theology, as their guides instead of searching the Scriptures to find for themselves how to live and believe.

The influence of the leading religious leaders led the Jewish nation to reject their Redeemer. The spirit that controlled those priests and rulers is still shown by many who act as if they are extremely religious. But they refuse to examine the Scriptures concerning the special truths for this time of earth's history. Instead, they point out how many they are, how wealthy, how popular—and scoff at those who maintain truth because they are few in number, poor, and unpopular, having a faith that separates them from the world.

Even though the Bible is full of warnings against false teachers, many people today depend on the clergy to define their spirituality. Thousands of church members can give no other reason for their beliefs than that is what they were taught by their religious leaders. They almost ignore Jesus' teachings and place total confidence in the words of the ministers. But are ministers perfect in their knowledge? How can we trust our spirituality to their guidance unless we know from God's Word that they are right? A lack of courage to stand alone leads many to follow highly educated professionals—by their reluctance to investigate for themselves, they are becoming hopelessly fastened in the chains of error.

Satan uses many influences to capture his victims. Many partner with Satan through their romantic attachments to those who are enemies of the cross of Christ. Parents, family, spouses, or friends who oppose Bible truth exert their power to control your conscience. Have courage to obey your own convictions!

It is impossible for us, with the Bible within our reach, to honor God by false opinions. You've probably heard that it doesn't matter what you believe, as long as your life is right. But your life is shaped by your faith. If truth is available to us and we choose to ignore it, we are choosing darkness.

"Sometimes there is a way that seems to be right, but in the end it is the way to death" (Proverbs 16:25). Ignorance is no excuse for sin when there is every opportunity to know the will of God. A young person on a road trip comes to an intersection with highway signs indicating where each freeway leads. If he ignores the signs and takes whichever road seems right to him, he may be completely sincere, but will likely find himself on the wrong road.

God has given us His Word so that we can become familiar with its teachings and know for ourselves what He requires of us. When the lawyer came to Jesus with the question "How am I saved?" Jesus referred him to the Scriptures, saying, "What is written in the law? What do you read there?" (Luke 10:26). Ignorance will not excuse young or old or release them from the punishment for breaking God's law when they could have understood its claims. It is not enough to have good intentions; it is not enough to do what you think is right or what the minister tells you is right. Your salvation is at stake, and you must search the Scriptures for yourself. However strong your convictions, however confident you may be that the minister knows what is truth, this is not your foundation. You have a chart pointing out every landmark on the trip to heaven, and you should not guess at anything.

Our first and highest duty is to learn from the Scriptures what is truth and then to obey what you learn and encourage others to do the same. We should study the Bible diligently every day, analyzing every thought, and comparing scripture with scripture. With divine help we are to form our opinions for ourselves, just as we are to answer for ourselves before God.

The truths that are most plainly revealed in the Bible have been covered in doubt and darkness by some theologians, who, pretending to be critical thinkers, teach that the Scriptures have a mystical, secret, spiritual meaning beyond the mere words. These people are false teachers. To this type of person Jesus declared, "You know neither the scriptures nor the power of God" (Mark 12:24). The language of the Bible should be explained according to its obvious meaning, unless a symbol or metaphor is used. Jesus has given the promise, "Anyone who resolves to do the will of God will know whether the teaching is from God" (John 7:17). If young people would take the Bible as it reads, if there were no false teachers to mislead and confuse their minds, a work would be accomplished that would make angels glad and that would bring thousands and thousands to Jesus who are now wandering in error.

We should discipline our minds to concentrate when we study the Scriptures. Even though we focus intently on understanding (within our human limitations) the deep things of

God, yet we must remember that the teachableness and submission of a child is the true spirit of the learner. Scriptural difficulties can never be mastered by the same methods used in grappling with philosophical problems. We should not come to the study of the Bible with that self-reliance with which many enter the domains of science, but with a prayerful dependence upon God and a sincere desire to learn His will. We must come with a humble and teachable spirit to receive knowledge from the God of the universe. Otherwise, evil angels will blind our minds and harden our hearts so that we will not be impressed with the truth.

An understanding of Bible truth doesn't depend as much on intellectual ability as on the intent, the earnest longing to do right.

The Bible should never be studied without prayer. Only the Holy Spirit can help us understand how important even the simple things are or prevent us from misinterpreting the difficult passages. The work of the heavenly angels is to prepare our hearts so to understand God's Word that we will be captivated by its beauty, cautioned by its warnings, and energized and strengthened by its promises. We should make the psalmist's prayer our own: "Open my eyes, so that I may behold wondrous things out of your law" (Psalm 119:18). Temptations often appear irresistible because, by neglecting prayer and the study of the Bible, we cannot quickly remember God's promises and meet Satan with the Scripture weapons. But angels surround those who are willing to be taught heaven's secrets, and in a crisis they will bring back to our minds the very truths that we need.

Jesus promised His disciples, "The Advocate, the Holy Spirit, whom the Father will send in my name, will teach you everything, and remind you of all that I have said to you" (John 14:26). But the teachings of Jesus must previously have been stored in our minds in order for the Spirit of God to bring them to our memory in the time of danger. "I treasure your word in my heart, so that I may not sin against you" (Psalm 119:11).

If you value your eternal interests, be on guard against the inroads of skepticism. The truth will be attacked. It is impossible to keep beyond the reach of sarcasm, fallacies, and subtle, destructive attitudes. Satan customizes his temptations to harass everyone. He attacks the illiterate with jokes or putdowns, while he meets the educated with scientific objections and philosophical reasoning. Both are premeditated to provoke distrust or contempt of the Scriptures. Even young people, with little of life's experience, sometimes presume to insinuate doubts concerning the basic principles of Christianity. Their skepticism, shallow as it is, influences others. Many are led to joke about the faith of their ancestors and cause pain to the Spirit of grace (Hebrews 10:29). Many lives that could have been an honor to God and a positive impact on the world have been spoiled by the foul breath of infidelity. All who trust to the bragging decisions of human reason and imagine that they can explain divine mysteries and arrive at truth unaided by the wisdom of God are entangled in the snare of Satan.

We are living in the most critical period of this world's history. The destiny of every person on Planet Earth is about to be decided. Our own future well-being, as well as the salvation of others, depends upon the course we now choose. We need to be guided by the Spirit of truth. Every follower of Christ should seriously ask, "Lord, what do You want me to do?" (Acts 9:6, NKJV). We should humble ourselves before the Lord with fasting and prayer and meditate much on His Word, especially on the scenes of the judgment. We should search for a living experience in the things of God. We don't have a moment to lose. Important, significant events are taking place around us; we are on Satan's enchanted ground. Don't sleep, sentries of God! The enemy is lurking near, waiting for you to become lazy and drowsy so he can spring upon you and make you his prey.

Are you deceived about your true condition before God? Do you congratulate yourself about the wrong acts you do not commit, and forget about the kind, compassionate deeds God requires and you have neglected to do? It is not enough to be trees in the garden of God. We are to meet God's expectations by bearing fruit. He holds us accountable for our failure to accomplish all the good that we could have done through His grace strengthening us. God doesn't want us to clutter up the garden. Yet even the case of the "clutterers" is not entirely hopeless. God's heart of patient love still pleads with those who have ignored God's mercy and abused His grace. " 'Sleeper, awake! Rise from the dead, and Christ will shine on you.' Be careful then how you live . . . making the most of the time" (Ephesians 5:14, 15).[118]

When the big test comes, those who have made God's Word their rule of life will be unveiled. In summer there is no noticeable difference between evergreens and other trees, but when the blasts of winter come, the evergreens remain unchanged while the other trees are stripped of their leaves. The superficial "Christian" may not now be easily distinguished from the real Christian, but the time is just upon us when the difference will be obvious. If opposition rises, if prejudice and intolerance occur, if persecution is kindled, the halfhearted and hypocritical will waver and yield the faith. But true Christians will stand firm as a rock, their faith stronger, their hope brighter than ever before![119]

Dear youth, pray as you never before prayed for beams from the Sun of Righteousness to shine upon the Word so that you may be able to understand its true meaning. Jesus pleaded that His disciples might live out their holy calling through the Word of God. You, then, should also intently pray that the Holy Spirit, our Guide to all truth, may be with you in your study of God's Holy Word.[120]

(For additional reading on this subject we recommend *The Great Controversy, Life Sketches, Experience and Teachings of Ellen G White,* and *Education.*)

Think About It

1. Briefly review the function of scripture as outlined in 2 Timothy 3:15-17. Which is easier and which is harder for you to include in you concept of inspiration?
2. If you were to discover an apparent discrepancy (difference) between the Bible and the writings of Ellen White, how would you go about resolving the issue?
3. What are several steps for preparing to study the Bible?
4. How does careful study of God's Word affect what we do in life?

ENDNOTES

Note: The material accompanying notes 1, 79, 82, 82, 87, 99, and 109 cite Ellen G White word for word. All other material paraphrases the Ellen G. White sources referenced.

Chapter 1: Beginnings

[1] *Christ's Object Lessons,* p. 118.
[2] *The Desire of Ages,* pp. 31, 32.
[3] *Ibid.,* p. 43.
[4] *Ibid.,* p. 44.
[5] *Ibid.,* p. 47.
[6] *Ibid.,* pp. 47, 48.
[7] *Ibid.,* p. 48.
[8] *Ibid.*
[9] *Ibid.,* pp. 48, 49

Chapter 2: Jesus as a Child and Young Adult

[10] *The Desire of Ages,* p. 84.
[11] *Ibid.,* p. 85.
[12] *Ibid.,* p. 86.
[13] *Ibid.,* p. 89.
[14] *Ibid.,* pp. 89, 90.
[15] *Ibid.,* pp. 87-91.
[16] *Ibid.,* p. 90.

Chapter 3: Jesus' Ministry Begins With a Party

[17] *The Desire of Ages,* p. 144.
[18] *Ibid.,* p. 145.
[19] *Ibid.*
[20] *Ibid.,* pp. 145, 146.
[21] *Ibid.,* p. 147.
[22] *Ibid.,* p. 148.
[23] *Ibid.,* pp. 148, 149.

Chapter 4: You Can Come Home Any Time

[24] *Christ's Object Lessons,* p. 198.
[25] *Ibid.,* pp. 199, 200.
[26] *Ibid.,* pp. 202, 203.

[27] *Ibid.*, pp. 203, 204.
[28] *Ibid.*, pp. 204, 205.
[29] *Ibid.*, pp. 205, 206.

Chapter 5: When Doing Everything Right Isn't Enough

[30] *The Desire of Ages,* pp. 518, 519.
[31] *Ibid.*, p. 519.
[32] *Ibid.*, p. 520.
[33] *Ibid.*, pp. 520, 523.
[34] *Ibid.*, p. 523.
[35] *Ibid.*, pp. 272, 273.
[36] *Ibid.*, p. 272.
[37] *Ibid.*
[38] *Ibid.*, pp. 273, 274.
[39] *Ibid.*, p. 275.
[40] *Ibid.*, p. 280.
[41] *Ibid.*

Chapter 6: The Answer Lies in the Soil

[42] *Christ's Object Lessons,* pp. 33, 34.
[43] *Ibid.*, pp. 34, 35.
[44] *Ibid.*, p. 35.
[45] *Ibid.*
[46] *Ibid.*, p. 38.
[47] *Ibid.*, p. 40.
[48] *Ibid.*, pp. 42-46.
[49] *Ibid.*, p. 47.
[50] *Ibid.*
[51] *Ibid.*, p. 49.
[52] *Ibid.*, pp. 49-52.
[53] *Ibid.*, pp. 58, 59.
[54] *Ibid.*, pp. 60, 61.
[55] *Ibid.*, p. 53-56.
[56] *Ibid.*, p. 47.

Chapter 7: How to Pray

[57] *Steps to Christ,* pp. 93, 94.
[58] *Ibid.*, pp. 94-96.
[59] *Ibid.*, p. 97.
[60] *Ibid.*, p. 98.
[61] *Ibid.*, pp. 101-103

Chapter 8: How to Have Faith

[62] *Steps to Christ,* pp. 49, 50.
[63] *Ibid.*, p. 51.
[64] *Steps to Christ,* p. 62.
[65] *Ibid.*, pp. 52, 53.

Chapter 9: Preparing to Die

[66] *The Desire of Ages,* pp. 685, 686.
[67] *Ibid.*, pp. 686-688.
[68] *Ibid.*, pp. 689, 690.
[69] *Ibid.*, p. 690.
[70] *Ibid.*, pp. 693-696.
[71] *Ibid.*, p. 697.

Chapter 10: Cruel Crucifixion

[72] *The Desire of Ages,* pp. 741-746.
[73] *Ibid.*, pp. 746-756.

Chapter 11: Grand Resurrection

[74] *The Desire of Ages,* pp. 779, 780.
[75] *Ibid.*, pp. 781, 782.
[76] *Ibid.*, pp. 788-790.
[77] *Ibid.*, p. 790.
[78] *Ibid.*, pp. 782-787.
[79] *The Acts of the Apostles,* p. 33.
[80] *Ibid.*, p. 27.

Chapter 12: How to Handle Doubts and Confusion

[81] *Steps to Christ,* pp. 105-113.

Chapter 13: Relationships

[82] *Patriarchs and Prophets,* p. 115.
[83] *Letters to Young Lovers,* pp. 25-27.
[84] *Ibid.*, pp. 21, 22.

Chapter 14: Wellness

[85] *In Heavenly Places,* p. 71.
[86] *Prophets and Kings,* pp. 479-483.
[87] *Ibid.*, pp. 483-486.
[88] *Ibid.*, pp. 488-490.

CHAPTER 15: SOCIAL JUSTICE

[89] *The Ministry of Healing,* pp. 17-19.
[90] *Testimonies to the Church,* vol. 2, pp. 25, 26.
[91] *The Desire of Ages,* p. 640.
[92] *Patriarchs and Prophets,* p. 534.
[93] *The Ministry of Healing,* p 187.
[94] *Ibid.,* p. 190.
[95] *Ibid.,* pp. 192, 193.
[96] *Ibid.,* p. 193.
[97] *Ibid.,* p. 195.
[98] *Ibid.,* pp. 194, 195.
[99] *Ibid.,* pp. 197, 198.
[100] *Patriarchs and Prophets,* pp. 534, 535.
[101] *The Desire of Ages,* p. 640.

CHAPTER 16: CAREERS

[102] *Christ's Object Lessons,* p. 327.
[103] *Fundamentals of Christian Education,* p. 82.
[104] Education, p. 262.
[105] *Ibid.,* p. 225.
[106] *Fundamentals of Christian Education,* p. 387.
[107] *Ibid.,* p. 358.
[108] *Education,* p. 267.
[109] *Ibid.,* pp. 268-270.
[110] *Ibid.,* pp. 263, 271.
[111] *Ibid.,* pp. 305, 306, 309.

CHAPTER 17: AUTHORITY OF SCRIPTURE

[112] *Colporteur Ministry,* p. 125.
[113] *Counsels to Teachers, Parents, and Students,* pp. 428, 429.
[114] *Ibid.,* p. 460.
[115] *Ibid.,* p. 53, 54.
[116] *My Life Today,* p. 283.
[117] *Counsels to Teachers, Parents, and Students,* p. 427.
[118] *The Great Controversy,* p. 601.
[119] *The Great Controversy,* pp. 593-602.
[120] *Testimony to Ministers,* p. 111.

CPSIA information can be obtained at www.ICGtesting.com
Printed in the USA
BVOW03s0353111213

338774BV00005B/7/P